EXPLANAT~~~
ROYAL COLLE
BC

MRCP (UK)
Part 1 papers
(February, June, October 1990)

HLC Beynon BSc MRCP
CN Ross MRCP

Department of Medicine, Hammersmith Hospital,
London

PASTEST

© 1992 PasTest
Egerton Court
Parkgate Estate,
Knutsford
Cheshire WA16 8DX

First published 1992
Reprinted 1993
Reprinted 1995
Reprinted 1997
Reprinted 1999

A catalogue record for this book is available from the British Library.

ISBN 0 906896 57 6

Printed by CRL Digital Print Services, Nottingham.

CONTENTS

PREFACE

This book contains detailed explanatory answers and teaching notes to the multiple choice questions in the Royal College of Physicians MRCP Part 1 Past Papers of February, June and October 1990. This book should be used alongside the Royal College publication since our text gives explanations to the Royal College answers and provides definitive lists for revision. Many of the topics are exam favourites and recur in successive papers. Exam technique is discussed in the Royal College publication.

H.L.C.B.
C.N.R.

Copies of the Royal College Green MCQ Booklet can be obtained from:
    The Royal College of Physicians
    11 St Andrews Place
    Regents Park
    LONDON NW1 4LE

Price £6.00 (incl. post & packing UK)
    £8.00 (incl. post & packing overseas)
    Prices correct at Jan 1997

COMMON PART I MRCP EXAMINATION PAPER
FEBRUARY 1990

(The correct answer options are given against each question.)

1. **CENTRAL CYANOSIS**   **ACD**

Cyanosis is the bluish colour imparted by deoxygenated or reduced haemoglobin. In practice, cyanosis can be detected when 2.6 g of reduced haemoglobin is present per 100 ml of blood, though most textbooks quote the figure of 5 g of reduced haemoglobin per 100 ml. Cyanosis may be central (reduced saturation of arterial blood) or peripheral (slow capillary circulation – increased extraction of oxygen) in origin. Methaemoglobinaemia and sulphaemoglobinaemia are also causes of cyanosis.

Causes of central cyanosis include
   Lung disease resulting in hypoxia
         e.g. lobar pneumonia, acute pancreatitis
   Heart disease with right to left shunt

Increasing the inspired oxygen concentration often improves the degree of cyanosis in cases of poor lung function, in contrast to cases of right to left shunting.

Causes of peripheral cyanosis include
   Atherosclerosis
   Vascular spasm
   Increased blood viscosity
   Low output cardiac failure

In cases of patent ductus arteriosus with secondary pulmonary hypertension, differential cyanosis may be present i.e. only the lower limbs are cyanosed. The phenomenon of orthocyanosis where cyanosis is only apparent in the upright position is associated with pulmonary arteriovenous malformations. Cyanosis is more marked in polycythaemic patients and is less marked in the presence of anaemia.

Methaemoglobinaemia is characterized by an increased amount of haemoglobin in which the iron is in the oxidized ferric form (Fe^{3+}).

1.5 g of methaemoglobin per 100 ml of blood produces an equivalent degree of central cyanosis to that seen with 5 g of reduced haemoglobin.

Causes of methaemoglobinaemia include
Congenital
   Red cell NADH — diaphorase deficiency
   Alpha or beta chain abnormality
Acquired
   Nitrites
   Nitrates
   Phenacetin
   Sulphonamides
   Primaquine
   Aniline dyes
   Chromate

Chronic methaemoglobinaemia (levels < 20%) is often well tolerated and may be associated with a mild haemolytic anaemia. The development of acute methaemoglobinaemia with large amounts of methaemoglobin (> 50%) is poorly tolerated and patients die of anoxia as methaemoglobin functions very poorly as an oxygen carrier (O_2 dissociation curve displaced to the left). Acute haemolysis and disseminated intravascular coagulation may complicate acute cases. Intravenous methylene blue is used to treat acute cases.

Carbon monoxide poisoning leads to the formation of carboxyhaemoglobin, which has an oxygen dissociation curve shifted strongly to the left. Carboxyhaemoglobin levels greater than 20% are associated with headaches and weakness. Levels in excess of 50% if untreated result in death. Carbon monoxide poisoning is characterized by pink mucus membranes and pink extremities. Today, inadequately ventilated heating appliances and car exhaust fumes (often suicide attempts) are the commonest causes of carbon monoxide poisoning.

2.   **OLECRANON BURSITIS**   BC

Inflammation of synovial bursae is common (bursitis). Olecranon bursitis is common and may be associated with excess elbow friction (beer drinker's elbow) or can complicate gout, rheumatoid arthritis or osteoarthritis.

Cholesterol containing olecranon bursae are seen in both rheumatoid and osteoarthritis but not primary cases of hypercholesterolaemia.

Rheumatological features of familial hypercholesterolaemia include a migratory polyarthritis and painful xanthomatous Achilles tendons.

3. **HYPONATRAEMIA**   **ADE**

Chlorpropamide and bronchial carcinoma are recognized causes of inappropriate anti-diuretic hormone secretion. Cirrhosis is one of the important causes of secondary hyperaldosteronism.

Causes of Hyponatraemia include:
   Pure water retention
      e.g. inappropriate antidiuretic hormone
   Retention of sodium and water with an excess of water
      e.g. nephrotic syndrome
      cirrhosis
      congestive heart failure
      Note: in these disease states total body sodium is increased
   Salt loss
      e.g. diuretic therapy
      Addison's disease
      salt losing nephropathy

Causes of Pseudohyponatraemia include:
   Hyperlipidaemia
   Hyperproteinaemia

Causes of Hypernatraemia include:
   Pure water deficiency
      e.g. diabctcs insipidus
   Hypotonic fluid loss
      e.g. urine losses
      sweating
      vomiting
      diarrhoea
   Salt gain
      e.g. mineralocorticoid excess
      intravenous hypertonic saline

Causes of syndrome of inappropriate anti-diuretic hormone (SIADH) secretion include
Malignancy
    e.g. oat cell carcinoma of the lung
    pancreatic carcinoma
    thymic carcinoma
    lymphoma
Drugs
    chlorpropamide
    carbamazepine
    chlorpromazine
    cyclophosphamide
    tricyclic antidepressants
    barbiturates
    bromocryptine
Neurological disease
    meningitis
    encephalitis
    cerebral abscess
    haematoma
    concussion/trauma
    acute intermittent porphyria
    Guillain-Barré syndrome
Respiratory disease
    pneumonia
    intermittent positive pressure ventilation

4.   HYPOKALAEMIC ACIDOSIS   BD

Distal renal tubular acidosis (Type 1) arises from an inability of the distal tubule to secrete H^+ ions. As a consequence of the H^+ retention there is a metabolic acidosis which is buffered by bone dissolution which results in hypercalcuria and thus nephrocalcinosis. The inability to secrete H^+ ions results in an increase in renal sodium loss, this stimulates aldosterone secretion which increases renal potassium loss. The classical metabolic abnormality accompanying renal tubule acidosis is a hyperchloraemic hypokalaemic metabolic acidosis. Clinical features include: failure to thrive, muscle weakness (hypokalaemia), osteomalacia, nephrocalcinosis and nephrolithiasis.

Causes of Distal Tubular Acidosis may be divided into
Congenital

Acquired
  Autoimmune disease
        e.g. Sjögren's syndrome
        chronic active hepatitis
        cryoglobulinaemia
  Nephrocalcinosis
        e.g. hyperparathyroidism,
        vitamin D intoxication
        medullary sponge kidney
  Drugs
        e.g. amphotericin
        analgesics
        lithium
  Renal disease
        e.g. transplanted kidney
        obstructive uropathy
        pyelonephritis

Fulminant ulcerative colitis may also be associated with a hypokalaemic metabolic acidosis.

5. CONGENITAL KIDNEY DISEASE   None correct

Infantile polycystic kidney disease is inherited as an autosomal recessive trait which manifests soon after birth and is usually fatal.

Adult polycystic kidney disease is an autosomal dominant trait, characterized by cystic dilation of any part of the nephron or collecting duct. Not all nephrons are affected but as the disease progresses normal nephrons become compressed by the enlarging cysts. Changes are present at birth but patients remain asymptomatic until adulthood. Clinical features include: abdominal pain, haematuria, palpable kidneys, infection, hypertension, renal stones, symptoms and signs of chronic renal failure and malignancy.

Medullary sponge kidney, characterized by multiple cystic dilations of the papillary collecting ducts has no clear mode of inheritance.

Patients are often asymptomatic and life expectancy is normal. Nephrocalcinosis may be apparent on the plain abdominal X-Ray and patients may develop related complications e.g. renal colic and infection.

Medullary cystic disease is characterized by clusters of cysts 1-10 mm in diameter at the corticomedullary junction. It may be inherited as an autosomal dominant or recessive trait and is a cause of chronic renal failure in young adults.

Nephrogenic diabetes insipidus is inherited in an X-linked recessive manner. The cells of the distal collecting duct and convoluted tubule are resistant to the effects of antidiuretic hormone. Affected males may present soon after birth with polyuria, dehydration and convulsions. Milder forms may present later with failure to thrive. If fluid intake can be increased to balance renal losses a normal life expectancy may be achieved. Thiazide diuretics have been used with good effect to induce a degree of hyponatraemia and reduce the chronic polyuria.

Alport's disease usually presents in childhood. There is no clear pattern of inheritance but males are affected more commonly and more severely than females. Haematuria is the commonest presenting feature, progressive renal failure usually occurs before the age of 25 years. High tone sensory neural deafness occurs in approximately one third of patients.

6.   SPINAL CORD TRANSECTION   BD

Following spinal cord transection there follows a period of spinal shock during which all spinal reflexes below the level of the transection are depressed.

Clinical features of a lower cervical transection include hypotonic paralysis (upper limbs will be spared), loss of sensation, paralysis of bladder and bowel function and profound hypotension with dry blue skin. As the stage of spinal shock resolves smooth muscle is the first to recover. Urinary sphincter tone returns to normal whilst the detrussor function is weak resulting in retention. Blood pressure recovers as the cell bodies of the vasoconstrictor fibres in the spinal cord function independently. Skeletal muscle tone returns after 2-3 weeks, the limbs adopting a position of slight flexion; spontaneous involuntary flexor movements of the limbs may occur. The autonomic reflexes eventually return allowing reflex evacuation of the bladder and bowels.

7.   **SEVENTH NERVE**   **BD**

The facial nerve leaves the pons at the cerebellopontine angle, and in close proximity to the eighth nerve enters the internal auditory canal and the facial canal which lies in the petrous temporal bone. The greater superficial petrosal nerve leaves at the geniculate ganglion and carries secretomotor fibres to the lacrimal gland. In the middle ear the facial nerve supplies motor fibres to the stapedius muscle. The facial nerve then leaves the petrous bone via the stylomastoid foramen, before doing so it gives off a branch the chorda tympani which carries taste from the anterior two thirds of the tongue and is secretomotor to the submandibular and sublingual glands, and a branch which supplies skin of the external auditory meatus. On exiting the stylomastoid foramen the nerve first supplies the stylohyoid and posterior belly of the digastric muscle before entering the parotid gland and dividing to supply the muscles of facial expression and platysma.

Note: Causes of ptosis do not include a facial nerve lesion.

8.   **INSULIN**   **ACD**

Insulin is secreted by the β cells of the pancreatic islets of Langerhans. It is initially synthesized as preproinsulin by the rough endoplasmic reticulum, this is then split to proinsulin which is packaged into secretory granules and the C-peptide part of the molecule is split off leaving the A and B polypeptide chains held by 2 cystine disulphide bridges. C-peptide is thus secreted in proportion to insulin. Insulin secretion in vivo is complex. Recognized stimuli include blood glucose levels (a calcium dependent process), glucagon, beta agonists (via an increase in c-AMP), amino acids, gut hormones (released in response to food in the intestine), fatty acids and vagal stimulation.

Insulin secretion thus rises prior to food consumption (vagal stimulation) this is followed by a steady rise in insulin concentration (gut hormones and blood glucose) as food is digested. This is maintained by the presence of absorbed amino acids. Plasma insulin levels return to baseline 2-3 hours after food consumption is finished. Basal insulin secretion is maintained by neuronal control and by fatty acids.

Certain types of obesity are characterized by insulin receptor resistance to circulating insulin e.g. HAIR-AN syndrome (hyperadrenalism, insulin resistance and acanthosis nigricans).

9. **DRUG INDUCED CONVULSIONS**   **BCDE**

    Drugs which can induce convulsions include
    Antihistamines
    Barbiturate withdrawal
    Phenothiazines
    Lignocaine
    High dose intrathecal penicillin
    Theophyllines
    Mefenamic acid
    Chlorpropamide
    Amitryptiline

10. **HYPOPHOSPHATAEMIA**   **BDE**

    Causes of hypophosphataemia include
    Hyperparathyroidism
    Treatment of diabetic ketoacidosis
    Alcoholism
    Vitamin D deficiency
    Proximal renal tubular acidosis
    Hypomagnesaemia
    Haemodialysis
    Hypothyroidism
    Respiratory or metabolic alkalosis
    Pregnancy
    Hungry bone syndrome (i.e. parathyroidectomy for hyperparathyroidism)
    Prolonged intravenous glucose administration.

Inappropriate use of phosphate binders in chronic renal failure
Acute liver failure

Hypoparathyroidism and rhabdomyolysis are associated with high phosphate levels.

11. MULTIPLE MYELOMA   **B**

Multiple myeloma is a neoplastic proliferation of plasma cells which results in
i)   a monoclonal protein in the serum and/or urine
ii) supression of normal serum immunoglobulin levels
iii) plasma cell accumulation in the marrow (> 10%)
iv) lytic bone lesions.

Most cases occur in those > 40 years. In 66% of cases the serum paraprotein is IgG, in 30% IgA and the rest are IgM or IgD. Bence-Jones proteins are present in 66% of cases. Clinical features include: bone pain, pathological fractures, symptoms of hypercalcaemia, repeated infections (serum immunoglobulin levels are decreased), abnormal bleeding and features of a hyperviscosity syndrome which results from polymerisation of immunoglobulins such as IgA, IgM and IgD. Investigations may show: a normochromic normocytic anaemia, high ESR, hypercalcaemia with a normal alkaline phosphatase unless pathological fractures are present, hyperuricaemia, hypoalbuminaemia and elevated urea and creatinine. In advanced stages leucopenia, thrombocytopenia and a leucoerythroblastic anaemia may be present. Alkylating agents such as cyclophosphamide or melphalan are used in combination with prednisolone. The median survival is 2 years, an elevated blood urea is a poor prognostic factor.

Differential diagnosis of a serum paraprotein
   Multiple myeloma
   Benign monoclonal gammopathy
   Macroglobulinaemia
   Lymphoma — rarely other carcinomas
   Chronic lymphatic leukaemia
   Chronic cold haemagglutinin disease

12. IMMUNOGLOBULIN G   CE

In normal serum IgG is present in a concentration of 8-16 mg/l, has a molecular weight of 150,000 and has a sedimentation coefficient of 7S. Like all antibody molecules, IgG is composed of 2 heavy chains (in the case of IgG γ chains) and 2 light chains (kappa or lambda) which are held together by disulphide bonds. Each IgG molecule has two antigen binding sites; papain will cleave IgG to yield 2 antigen binding sites (Fab fragments) and 1 Fc fragment.

IgG is the major immunoglobulin synthesized during a secondary immune response. IgG is the predominant immunoglobulin found in the extracellular space and is of primary importance in binding to microorganisms, activating the classical complement pathway and enhancing their phagocytosis. IgG is the only immunoglobulin which crosses the placenta and maternal IgG is responsible for protecting the newborn against infection. Paradoxically maternal IgG may be responsible for certain autoimmune diseases in the neonate e.g. myasthenia gravis, autoimune idiopathic thrombocytopenia purpura, Grave's disease and congenital heart block (mother with SLE who is Ro antibody positive).

IgM molecules (molecular weight 900,000) are pentamers of four peptide subunits (i.e. 2 heavy, 2 light chains) which theoretically have an antigen valency of 10 but in practice a valency of 5. IgM is primarily confined to the blood and these molecules are the first to be produced in a primary immune response. They are very effective in agglutinating microrganisms, and fit complement to aid phagocytosis. The natural haemagglutinins (anti-A and anti-B) are usually IgM antibodies which are cold antibodies i.e. they react best at room temperature.

IgE (molecular weight of 200,000) is found in low concentrations in the serum and is involved in Type 1 hypersensitivity (anaphylactic) reactions. It is found attached to mast cells in the skin. Serum IgE levels are high in patients with parasitic infestations, fungal infections and allergic reactions to pollens, drugs and foreign antigens.

IgD (molecular weight of 185,000) is present mainly on the surface of blood lymphocytes where it operates as a receptor.

IgA is discussed in question 12, June 1990.

13. **TUBERCULOSIS**   **ACE**

Erythema nodosum complicates between 1-15% of cases of primary tuberculosis and is invariably associated with a strongly positive tuberculin test.

Tuberculosis is a recognized complication of silicosis a fibrotic lung disease due to crystalline silicone dioxide inhalation. Interestingly silicosis is also associated with an increased incidence of autoimmune disease such as rheumatoid arthritis and systemic lupus erythematosus.

Uveitis is a recognized complication of tuberculosis either as a consequence of mycobacterial infection or as a secondary immunological reaction.

Ocular complications of tuberculosis include
    Uveitis
    Choroidal tubercules a feature of miliary tuberculosis
    Phylctenular conjunctivitis — small yellow conjunctival nodules near
    the limbus is a recognized complication of primary tuberculosis
    and usually occurs within a year of the primary infection.

Chronic carriage of hepatitis B has been associated with polyarteritis nodosa.

Recognized causes of uveitis include
    Sarcoidosis
    Seronegative arthritides
        e.g. Still's disease, ankylosing spondylitis, Reiter's syndrome
    Vasculitides
        e.g. Behçet's disease
    Infections
        e.g. tuberculosis, syphilis, toxoplasmosis, toxocara, herpes zoster
    Acquired immune deficiency syndrome
    Vogt-Koyanagi-Harada syndrome (common in Japan)
    Bowel disease
        e.g. Crohn's disease, Whipple's disease
    Multiple sclerosis

Note: Ocular disease is a rare complication of ulcerative colitis.

14. MATERNAL INFECTIONS   CDE

Primary maternal toxoplasma infection in early pregnancy may lead to fetal death. Clinical features of congenital toxoplasmosis include: microcephaly, cerebral calcification, low I.Q., cerebral convulsions, spasticity and chorioretinitis.

Primary maternal infection with rubella in the first 2 months of pregnancy is associated with a 50% risk of congenital abnormality this falls to a 20% risk between the third and fourth months.

Clinical features of congenital rubella include:
  Gregg's triad of i) cardiovascular defects e.g. patent ductus
  arteriosus, Fallot's tetralogy and pulmonary stenosis,
  ii) sensorineural deafness and iii) eye defects e.g. cataracts,
  retinopathy, glaucoma and microphthalmus.
  Thrombocytopenia, hepatitis, meningo-encephalitis and growth
  retardation are also common.

Primary maternal cytomegalovirus infection in pregnancy can lead to fetal abnormalities, which include: hepato-splenomegaly, jaundice, purpura, microcephaly, intracranial calcification, cerebral palsy, deafness, cataracts, hydrocephalus and congenital heart disease.

15. MEASLES/MUMPS/RUBELLA VACCINE   BC

The MMR vaccine (a freeze dried preparation) should be given to children of 12-18 months, with the aim of preventing all three viral infections. Until the first cohort of children vaccinated before the age of 2 years reach school, the vaccine should also be given to children at school entry i.e. less than 5 years of age. Until this immunization strategy is effective the policy of immunizing girls 10-14 years of age with rubella vaccine will continue. MMR vaccine should be given irrespective of previous history of measles, mumps or rubella. Contraindications to the use of the vaccine include:
  i)   untreated malignancy
  ii)   immunosuppressive treatment
  iii) hypogammaglobulinaemia
  iv)   known history of anaphylaxis e.g. to egg or allergies to
        neomycin or kanamycin

neomycin or kanamycin
v) MMR vaccine should not be given during an acute febrile
illness or within 3 months of a previous immunoglobulin
injection. MMR vaccine should be given under close
supervision if there is either a history or close family history of
convulsions and appropriate advice offered about treatment of
fevers which may follow vaccination.

Recognized side effects of MMR vaccination include: fever and rash
maximal 7 days post vaccination, and mild parotid swelling.

The DHSS recommendations are that HIV positive children should
receive MMR vaccine. HIV positive children should also receive
inactivated polio vaccine, whooping cough, diptheria, tetanus, and
hepatitis B vaccine, but BCG is contraindicated as there have been
reports of disseminated tubercle.

16. ANTIMICROBRIAL TREATMENT FOR GASTROINTESTINAL INFECTIONS   CE

Giardia lamblia is a flagellate parasite found throughout the world but
is common in the tropics and Eastern Europe. Man is infected by
ingesting cysts in contaminated food or inadequately treated drinking
water. Asymptomatic cyst excretors are recognized. Symptomatic
infection may manifest as an acute or chronic illness. The acute illness
has an incubation period of approximately two weeks, clinical features
include: foul smelling diarrhoea, nausea, weight loss and mild fever.
Chronic cases may present with diarrhoea, lactose intolerance, weight
loss and failure to thrive. The diagnosis is confirmed by finding cysts
in the faeces or demonstrating the flagellate trophozoites in jejunal
aspirate or jejunal biopsy (which may show subtotal villous atrophy).
Oral metronidazole is the treatment of choice.

Pseudomembranous colitis, an exudative infection of the large bowel
is caused by the exotoxin of the anaerobic spore forming rod
Clostridium difficile. It is usually seen as a complication of antibiotic
therapy (commonly lincomycin, clindamycin and ampicillin) but may
also complicate colonic carcinoma and uraemia. Fit individuals rarely
carry *Clostridium difficile*. Antibiotic therapy alters the normal gut
commensal organisms facilitating *C. difficile* colonization. Clinical

features vary from mild diarrhoea to severe debilitation complicated by a toxic megacolon. The diagnosis may be confirmed by finding *C. difficile* toxin in the stool. Sigmoidoscopy may show the classical yellow exudative plaques, histologically there is evidence of mucosal necrosis with a fibrinous exudate rich in neutrophils. Cases should be treated with oral vancomycin or oral metronidazole.

The majority of cases of Salmonella gastroenteritis (*Salmonella enteritidis, typhimurium* and *heidelberg*) respond to rehydration and supportive measures. Antibiotics should not be used and in many cases actually prolong excretion of the organism. Cases of enteric fever (Salmonella typhi or paratyphi A and B) should be treated with chloramphenicol, amoxycillin or co-trimoxazole.

Campylobacter gastroenteritis (*Campylobacter jejuni* and *coli*) typically has an incubation period of 3 days — range 1 to 7 days. Asymptomatic carriage in children is common, clinical features may vary from a mild self-limiting episode of diarrhoea to a severe debilitating illness with marked abdominal pain and bloody diarrhoea. Prodromal influenza symptoms with a high fever, myalgias and arthralgias are common. Severe cases of Campylobacter gastroenteritis may be treated with erythromycin, gentamicin or chloramphenicol. The majority require rehydration and supportive measures.

The successful treatment of cholera depends on prompt rehydration and electrolyte replacement. When oral rehydration is undertaken it is essential that the fluid contains glucose. Cholera enterotoxin impairs the mucosal absorption of neutral sodium chloride but has no effect on glucose facilitated sodium chloride transport. Antibiotics (tetracyclines, furazolidine and chloramphenicol) have been shown to reduce the duration of the diarrhoea and facilitate vibrio eradication but are not essential.

17. INEFFECTIVE ERYTHROPOIESIS ACD

Addisonian pernicious anaemia, folic acid deficiency and sideroblastic anaemia are all characterized by increased bone marrow erythropoietic activity.

Aplastic anaemia due to indomethacin and Fanconi anaemia are characterized by decreased marrow erythropoietic activity.

Aplastic anaemia is defined as pancytopenia resulting from marrow hypoplasia characterized by a decrease in the number of pluripotent stem cells.

Causes of Aplastic Anaemia include
Primary
congenital-Fanconi anaemia
idiopathic acquired
Secondary causes
drugs e.g. alkylating agents, chloramphenicol, gold, NSAIDs
infections e.g. infectious hepatitis
radiation
chemicals e.g. organic solvents, insecticides

Fanconi anaemia is inherited as an autosomal recessive trait. Pancytopenia develops at approximately five years of age, associated clinical features include hyperpigmentation; short stature; hypoplasia of the radius, thumb and carpus; microsomy; microcephaly; kidney malformation; mental retardation and hypogonadism. The disorder is characterized by multiple chromosomal breaks and aberrations. Bone marrow transplantation is curative but success rates are low.

Sideroblastic anaemia is characterized by ring sideroblasts in the marrow; there is defective utilization of iron and impaired haem synthesis. Typically serum iron and ferritin levels are raised and total iron binding capacity normal.

Causes of sideroblastic anaemia include
Congenital X-linked recessive
Acquired
primary
myeloproliferative disorders
drugs e.g. alcohol, isoniazid and lead

Addisonian pernicious anaemia and folic acid deficiency are causes of megaloblastic anaemia — the bone marrow is hypercellular with large erythroblasts showing delay in nucleus maturation.

Addisonian pernicious anaemia has a peak age of onset of 60 years, a female to male ratio 1.5:1, is seen more commonly in Northern Europeans (associated with blue eyes, grey hair and blood group A), and is associated with other autoimmune diseases. Overall there is an increased incidence of gastric carcinoma. Typically there is gastric atrophy with subsequent achlorhydria and lack of intrinsic factor which results in B_{12} deficiency. 90% of patients have anti-parietal cell antibodies but these are non-specific, 50% have antibodies which block intrinsic factor binding to B_{12} and 35% have antibodies which block the intrinsic factor-B_{12} complex from binding to specific receptors in the terminal ileum. Non-haematological features of B_{12} deficiency include subacute combined degeneration of the cord, a symmetrical peripheral neuropathy, optic neuritis, glossitis, angular chelitis, mild jaundice, and when severe, purpuric lesions due to thrombocytopenia. The anaemia is macrocytic with a hypercellular marrow, the platelet and neutrophil counts may be depressed; classically the neutrophils are hypersegmented (a right shift). Serum unconjugated bilirubin levels, LDH and hydroxybutyrate are all increased. Vitamin B_{12} levels are low, serum folic acid levels are normal or elevated and red cell folate levels are normal or low.

The Schilling test will distinguish Addisonian pernicious anaemia from B_{12} deficiency secondary to terminal ileal disease. Addisonian pernicious anaemia should be treated with intramuscular hydroxycobalamin.

Causes of B_{12} deficiency include
   Addisonian pernicious anaemia
   Veganism (animal produce is the main source of B_{12})
   Gastrectomy
   Congenital lack of intrinsic factor
   Terminal ileal resection
   Ileal disease e.g. Crohn's disease
   Ileal bacterial overgrowth — blind loop syndrome, chronic tropical
      sprue
   Rare causes include; metformin, phenformin, fish tapeworm and
      coeliac disease

18. ACUTE INTERMITTENT PORPHYRIA   **ABD**

The porphyrias are a family of diseases which result from enzyme deficiencies in the haem biosynthetic pathway. All porphyrias with the exception of acute intermittent porphyria show photosensitivity. Acute intermittent porphyria is inherited in an autosomal dominant manner and usually presents in the late twenties. Females are affected more commonly than males.

Clinical features include:
Abdominal pain, vomiting, constipation
Peripheral neuropathy (usually a symmetrical myopathy, trunk and
    respiratory muscle weakness can occur)
Depression, hysteria and psychotic symptoms.
Grand mal epilepsy
Fever
Sinus tachycardia and hypertension
Papilloedema,
Hyponatraemia due to increased antidiuretic hormone secretion
Leucocytosis

Acute intermittent porphyria is characterized by raised levels of delta amino laevulinic acid and porphobilinogen in the urine which are further increased during an acute attack. The urine turns red/brown on standing and the diagnosis may be confirmed by detection of excess porphobilinogen in the urine using Ehrlich's aldehyde reagent — a pink colour which is insoluble in chloroform or butanol is obtained.
Factors known to precipitate an attack include
    i)   menstruation
    ii) pregnancy
    iii) infection
    iv) dieting
    v)   alcohol
    vi) drugs e.g. sulphonamides, anticonvulsants (barbiturates,
         phenytoin), griseofulvin and the contraceptive pill.

19. COOMBS' TEST   **ACD**

The direct Coombs' test detects antibody or complement on the surface of red blood cells. Red blood cells are mixed with either anti-IgG, anti-IgM, anti-IgA, anti-C3 or anti-C4. Red cell agglutination indicates a positive test.

Causes of a positive Coombs' test include
    Autoimmune haemolytic disease
    Drug induced autoimmune haemolytic disease
    Haemolytic disease of the newborn
    Haemolytic transfusion reactions

Autoimmune haemolytic anaemia may be divided into warm and cold types.

Warm autoimmune haemolytic anaemia, is typically associated with IgG autoantibodies which are best detected at $37^{o}C$.

Causes of a warm autoimmune haemolytic anaemia include
    Idiopathic
    Secondary
        systemic lupus erythematosus
        lymphomas
        chronic lymphatic leukaemia
        drugs

Red blood cells coated with IgG are taken up by splenic reticuloendothelial cells which remove part of the red cell membrane resulting in spherocytosis. Splenomegaly is often a feature. The underlying cause should be treated where appropriate. High dose prednisolone is often effective and splenectomy may be of value.

Cold autoimmune haemolytic anaemia is typically associated with IgM autoantibodies which are best detected at $4^{o}C$.

Causes of a cold autoimmune haemolytic anaemia include
    Idiopathic
    Secondary
        lymphomas
        mycoplasma infection
        infectious mononucleosis
        paroxysmal nocturnal haemoglobinaemia

The autoantibody binds best to red cells in the periphery and is usually directed against the I antigen. The degree of haemolysis depends on the antibody affinity and its ability to bind complement. Impaired capillary perfusion may complicate peripheral agglutination. Treatment is directed against the underlying cause and attention paid to maintaining peripheral body temperature.

Drug induced haemolytic anaemia may be divided into 3 groups
1) Antibody directed against a drug — red cell membrane complex — usually IgG e.g. penicillin.

2) Immune complex formation with complement deposition on the red cells e.g. phenacetin, antimalarials, sulphonamides.

3) Autoimmune — usually IgG, e.g. methyldopa, mefenamic acid.

Note: The indirect Coombs' test is used to detect blood group antibodies in the serum.

20. OESTROGEN CONTAINING CONTRACEPTIVE PILL   ACD

Recognized side effects of the oral contraceptive pill include: nausea, headaches, breast tenderness, weight gain, chloasma, breakthrough bleeding, post-pill amenorrhoea, loss of libido, mood change, migraines, impaired glucose tolerance, intolerance of contact lenses.

Venous thrombosis, stroke, myocardial infarction, hypertension, jaundice, gallstones and liver tumours including haemangiomas are recognized complications.

The oral contraceptive pill should be avoided in the following conditions: porphyria, hepatic disease (including chronic active hepatitis, biliary cirrhosis, Dubin-Johnson and Rotor syndromes), cancers of the breast and urinary tract and other oestrogen dependent tumours, severe migraine, a history of previous thrombo-embolic disease, stroke, ischaemic heart disease, hyperlipidaemia and hypertension.

The contraceptive pill should be used with caution in patients with sickle cell disease and systemic lupus erythematosus.

21. FOLIC ACID DEFICIENCY   ABCE

Man cannot synthesize folic acid; bacteria on the other hand synthesize folic acid from para-aminobenzoic acid, pteridine and glutamic acid. 5,10 methylene-tetrahydrofolate is required for the synthesis of thymidine monophosphate a component of DNA from deoxyuridine monophosphate a reaction regulated by the enzyme thymidylate synthesase. During the synthesis of thymidine monophosphate 5,10 methylene-tetrahydrofolate is oxidized to the functionally inactive dihydrofolate. Regeneration of the active 5,10 methylene-tetrahydrofolate requires the enzyme dihydrofolate reductase. Methotrexate is an antimetabolite which inhibits dihydrofolate reductase, blocking the synthesis of DNA. Similarly pyrimethamine a weaker antagonist will also inhibit the enzyme dihydrofolate reductase. Trimethoprim has a similar action and in combination with a sulphonamide (a structural analogue of para-aminobenzoic acid) will inhibit bacterial folic acid synthesis. Methotrexate or pyrimethamine toxicity may be reversed by giving the patient a stable fully reduced form of folate − folinic acid.

Anticonvulsants e.g. phenytoin and barbiturates are recognized causes of folic acid deficiency − the exact mechanism is undetermined.

Common causes of Folic acid deficiency include
   Poor oral intake − greens and liver are a rich source
   Malabsorption e.g. coeliac disease, tropical sprue, Crohn's disease
   Excess utilization-prematurity, malignancy, psoriasis
   Phenytoin therapy
   Liver disease and heart failure lead to increased urine folate loss

   Note: Peritoneal dialysis and haemodialysis have been associated with folic acid deficiency.

22. DRUG INDUCED JAUNDICE   ABD

Abnormalities of liver function tests and jaundice are common side effects of many drugs. Drugs causing jaundice may be divided into those causing a primary hepatitic picture and those causing a predominantly cholestatic one.

Hepatitis like reactions
Halothane and monoamine-oxidase inhibitors (both dose independent)
Isoniazid

Cholestasis with a hepatitic component
Phenothiazines e.g. chlorpromazine
Chlorpropamide
Tricyclic antidepressants
Benzodiazepines
Anti-TB drugs e.g. PAS, rifampicin, pyrazinamide, ethambutol
Antibiotics e.g. erythromycin (estolate), fusidic acid sulphonamides
Oestrogens (pure cholestasis)
Methyltestosterone derivatives
Note: Paracetamol toxicity is associated with hepatic necrosis.

23. DIABETES INSIPIDUS   AB

Causes of diabetes insipidus include
1. Cranial diabetes insipidus
Congenital
DIDMOAD syndrome (diabetes insipidus, diabetes mellitus, optic atrophy and deafness)

Acquired
    idiopathic
    trauma
    tumour
    ischaemia e.g. Sheehan's syndrome
    infections
    granulomatous disease

2. Nephrogenic diabetes insipidus
Congenital — an X-linked recessive trait

Acquired
    hypokalaemia
    hypercalcaemia
    lithium toxicity
    amphotericin

demeclocycline/and outdated tetracyclines
glibenclamide

Drugs used in the treatment of diabetes insipidus include
dDAVP — desmopressin(nasal spray); the drug of choice for cranial
diabetes insipidus.

Thiazide diuretics are the drug of choice for nephrogenic diabetes
insipidus by inducing mild sodium depletion they reduce urine volume.
Chlorpropamide has two actions, it stimulates antidiuretic hormone
secretion and also potentiates the action of antidiuretic hormone on
the distal convoluted tubule and collecting duct.
Carbamazepine and clofibrate have both been shown to stimulate
antidiuretic hormone secretion.
The biguanides have an antidiuretic action in hypokalaemic
nephrogenic diabetes insipidus.
Non steroidal anti-inflammatory agents reduce urine volumes in both
cranial and nephrogenic diabetes insipidus.

Note: The clinical features of antidiuretic hormone deficiency
accompanying hypopituitarism may be altered by the antidiuretic
action of cortisol deficiency (exact mechanism unknown).

With complete ADH deficiency urine volumes may reach 10-20 litres
(urine osmolality 50-100 mosmol/kg). Hypernatraemia does not occur
provided the thirst mechanism is intact and the patient has access to
water.

24. GOUT   ACDE

Recognized causes of hyperuricaemia include
1. Increased synthesis of uric acid
   Primary gout (25%)
   Lesh Nyhan syndrome
   Disease states characterized by a high cell turnover e.g.
   myeloproliferative disorders, psoriasis

2. Decreased uric acid excretion
   Primary gout (70%)
   Hyperparathyroidism

Lead nephropathy (renal tubule damage)
Down's syndrome
Exercise
Starvation
Alcohol
Toxaemia of pregnancy
Glucose 6 phosphate dehydrogenase deficiency
Hyperlipidaemia
Drugs — low dose salicylates, diuretics, ethambutol, pyrazinamide

Mild levels of hyperuricaemia per se require no treatment. Uric acid levels persistently > 0.6 mmol/l and hyperuricaemia associated with renal impairment should be treated.

Colchicine or indomethacin are recognized first line agents in the management of acute gout.

Hypouricaemic therapy should be introduced for the following: three or more attacks of acute gout, hyperuricaemia and associated renal impairment, uric acid stones tophi and the presence of bone destruction. Drugs used in the management of chronic hyperuricaemia include allopurinol a xanthine oxidase inhibitor and drugs which have a uricosuric action e.g. probenecid, sulphinpyrazone and azapropazone which are particularly useful in uric acid undersecretors.

There is a marked increase in the incidence of acute attacks of gout in the first couple of months following the introduction of hypouricaemic agents and colchicine prophylaxis (0.5 mg b.d.) should be utilised.

Note: High dose aspirin has a uricosuric action, low/normal dosages are associated with an increase in serum uric acid levels.

25. CLINICAL DRUG TRIAL   ADE

The process of stratification reduces the effects of chosen baseline parameters e.g. the population may be divided into different strata for age and sex and random samples may then be taken from each group.

Randomization ensures that the allocation of treatment to each patient is a matter of chance but randomized allocation to different treatment groups does not eliminate baseline variables. Increasing the number of patients allocated to each treatment group will reduce the effect of baseline differences.

The null hypothesis assumes that there is no statistically significant difference in the response between the different groups.

26. INDUSTRIAL LUNG DISEASE   E

Coalworker's pneumoconiosis is due to inhalation of coalmine dust. The pathogenicity depends on
  i)   the compostion of the 0.5-7 μm spheres — high quartz and high carbon dusts are particularly harmful
  ii)   the amount of dust which reaches acinar level.

Simple pneumoconiosis is asymptomatic. Clinical examination is normal and the chest X-ray shows small 1-5 mm opacities maximal in the mid and upper zones and sometimes irregular opacities in the lower zones. It predisposes the individual to progressive massive fibrosis a complication which may occur many years after exposure to coal dust ceases. Progressive massive fibrosis is associated with a restrictive lung defect (often complicated by a degree of emphysema) which leads to cor pulmonale and death. The chest X-ray shows fibrosis initially in the upper zone, and cavitation may be a feature. Coalminer's pneumoconiosis is not associated with
  i)   finger clubbing
  ii)   an increased risk of lung malignancy
  iii) an increased risk of tuberculosis.

Caplan's syndrome is the syndrome of rheumatoid arthritis and the presence of several 1-5 cm lung nodules (which may cavitate) in a coalminer with pneumoconiosis; histologically they are similar to rheumatoid nodules. If a coalminer develops simple pneumoconiosis he should be moved to a job with low dust exposure and should be assessed for disablement benefits.

Asbestosis (pulmonary fibrosis) arises from exposure to asbestos fibres (chrysotile, crocidolite and amosite; $>3\mu$m diameter and $>10\mu$m in length).

All types are associated with asbestosis, pleural plaques and an increased risk of lung cancer; crocidolite and amosite are associated with an increased risk of mesothelioma. Asbestosis does not predispose to tuberculosis. Clinical features of asbestosis include cough, progressive shortness of breath, a restrictive lung defect, finger clubbing and the chest X-ray shows predominantly basal fibrosis.

Pleural plaques are usually asymptomatic. Up to 50% of smokers with asbestosis die of bronchial carcinoma.

A history of previous asbestos exposure may be obtained from 90% of patients with a mesothelioma. Average survival after mesothelioma diagnosis is 8 months.

Isocyanates are used in the manufacture of polyurethanes. Acute toxicity from isocyanate exposure (as seen in the Indian Bhopal disaster, 1984) is associated with lacrimation, sore throat, corneal ulcers, and pulmonary oedema (**Note:** at variance with college answer). Treatment for acute exposure is supportive. Isocyanates are a recognized cause of occupational induced asthma and affected individuals are entitled to industrial compensation. Occupational asthma is defined as asthma which develops after a variable period of symptomless exposure to a sensitizing agent encountered at work.

Allergens in various organic dusts give rise to extrinsic allergic alveolitis which is associated with the presence of precipitating antibodies in the blood. Farmer's lung and the related silo-fillers' lung follow the inhalation of dust from mouldy hay which harbours the *Micropolyspora faeni* antigen.

Acute exposure to cadmium fumes is associated with a pneumonitis. Chronic cadmium exposure (alloy and battery manufacture) is associated with an increased risk of emphysema.

27. ARTHRITIS   ABCE

Yersinia enterocolitica is one of the organisms implicated in the post dysenteric form of Reiter's syndrome. Other organisms include *Shigella dysenteriae, Shigella flexneri, Salmonella*, and *Campylobacter jejeuni*. The post venereal form is associated with *Mycoplasma* and

Chlamydia. Reiter's syndrome is strongly linked with HLA B27 and males are affected more commonly than females. Clinical features of acute Reiter's include the classic triad of arthritis (asymmetrical oligoarthritis predominantly affecting the lower limbs), conjunctivitis and urethritis. Other clinical features include: enthesopathy, keratoderma blenorrhagica, circinate balanitis, apthous ulcers, nail dystrophy and fever. 60% of patients develop chronic symptoms which include: arthritis, uveitis, cardiac conduction defects, aortic regurgitation, pericarditis, peripheral neuropathy and transient pulmonary infiltrates.

Whipple's disease is a rare disorder characterized by the presence of PAS positive 'foamy' macrophages in many tissues including the small intestine, lymph nodes and synovium. Clinical features include a predeliction for caucasian males aged 25-50 years, recurrent attacks of self limiting migratory arthritis predominantly affecting the knees and ankles, fever, malabsorption, weight loss, diarrhoea, hyperpigmentation, clubbing, hepatosplenomegaly, lymphadenopathy, pericarditis and pleurisy. The joint symptoms predominate in the early part of the illness. The aetiology is unknown but an infective cause has been postulated and this is supported by the response to prolonged therapy with tetracyclines.

Pyoderma gangrenosum (classically a well demarcated ulcer with a necrotic base and an overhanging purple edge) has a well recognized association with rheumatoid arthritis, ulcerative colitis, Crohn's disease, Wegener's granulomatosis and plasma cell dyscrasias. A bullous form of pyoderma is associated with leukaemia.

Note: The college answer acknowledges an association between coeliac disease and arthritis. This association is subject to debate and probably relates to the recognized association between coeliac disease and other autoimmune disorders which are associated with the haplotype A1 B8 DR3 e.g. systemic lupus erythematosus.

28. SYSTEMIC LUPUS ERYTHEMATOSUS   ABCD

Systemic lupus erythematosus (SLE) is a multisystem disease of unknown aetiology which is characterized by autoantibodies to DNA and other cell nucleus antigens. Women are affected more commonly than men, with a peak age of onset of 20-30 years.

Clinical features of active SLE include
Fever
Arthritis
Rashes
Raynaud's phenomenon
Alopecia
Apthous ulcers
Serositis (pleurisy and pericarditis)
Nephritis
     minimal change
     membranous
     mesangiocapillary
     focal and diffuse proliferative
Neuropsychiatric disease
Haematological abnormalities
     haemolytic anaemia — positive Coombs'
     leucopenia
     lymphopenia
     thrombocytopenia
Immunological abnormalities
     Positive ANA
     Positive anti-dsDNA antibodies
     Positive anti-ENA antibodies (Sm, RNP, Ro and La)
     Low complement levels
     Anti-phospholipid antibodies (positive VDRL)
     Lupus anticoagulant
     Hypergammaglobulinaemia
Acute phase response
     Elevated ESR and normal CRP

The haematoxylin body (tissue equivalent of the LE cell) is characteristic of SLE. The onion skin lesion due to marked perivascular fibrosis around central and peripheral splenic arteries is one of the most characteristic pathological changes in SLE. Other typical pathological findings in SLE include fibrinoid necrosis, particulary affecting small arteries and arterioles, eosinophilic thickening of kidney basement membrane capillary loops — the so called wire loops, immune complex deposition in the kidney, follicular plugging and scarring characteristic of discoid lupus, the demonstration of immunoglobulin and complement along the dermo-epidermal junction in both lesional and non lesional skin (lupus band test) and Libman-Sachs endocarditis.

The commonest pulmonary complication of SLE is pleurisy. Other recognized complications include: elevation of the diaphragms (shrinking lung syndromes), pneumonitis, recurrent atelectasis, diffuse lung infiltrates and pulmonary fibrosis.

29. DRESSLER'S SYNDROME   ABCE

Dressler's syndrome complicates between 1-5% of myocardial infarctions (two to eight weeks post infarction) and is also seen after cardiac surgery. Clinical features include; fever, pericarditis, pleurisy, fever, normochromic normocytic anaemia and an elevated ESR; cardiac tamponade is rare. It is thought to be immunologically mediated and anti- heart muscle antibodies have been demonstrated.

Non-steroidal anti-inflammatory agents are usually effective, though corticosteroids are often required for severe or refractory cases. It tends to be a chronic condition and treatment may need to continue for several months.

Anticoagulating a patient with pericarditis may result in pericardial haemorrhage and possibly tamponade.

30. SPLITTING OF THE SECOND HEART SOUND   BC

The second heart sound arises from closure of the aortic and pulmonary valves at the end of ventricular systole. During expiration the aortic and pulmonary components of the second sound are all but inseparable. Splitting of the second heart sound may be heard in children and young adults on inspiration as the increased venous return delays closure of the pulmonary valve in comparison with the aortic valve.

Fixed splitting of the second heart sound is pathognomonic of an atrial septal defect — the left to right shunt results in an increase in right ventricular stoke volume which splits the second sound and because the right and left atria are in communication the splitting is fixed. Any process which delays closure of the pulmonary valve relative to the aortic valve will result in a split second sound e.g. right bundle branch block and pulmonary stenosis.

Splitting of the second sound is not a feature of pulmonary hypertension because the ejection time of the right ventricle is not delayed.

Reversed splitting of the second sound will occur if the aortic component is delayed and is seen in hypertrophic obstructive cardiomyopathy and cases of aortic stenosis (with a pliable valve).

Fallot's tetralogy is the commonest cause of cyanotic congenital heart disease after 1 year of age. The tetralogy as originally described consisted of
   i)   pulmonary stenosis
   ii) VSD
   iii) over-riding aorta
   iv) right ventricular hypertrophy.
Additional anomalies since described include: aortic regurgitation and absent left pulmonary artery. Patients present with cyanosis from 3-6 months, other clinical features include growth retardation, cyanotic attacks, infective endocarditis, cerebral abscess, paradoxical embolism and symptoms of polycythaemia. Physical signs include: clubbing, polycythaemia, right ventricular hypertrophy, palpable aortic component of second heart sound, single second heart sound (aortic only) and an ejection systolic murmur associated with a thrill at the left sternal edge. Squatting, by increasing the degree of systemic vascular resistance, reduces the degree of cyanosis by increasing pulmonary flow and reducing the right to left shunt. Chest X-ray shows the coeur en sabot appearance (heart in a boot) with oligaemic lung fields and small pulmonary arteries. ECG abnormalities include right axis deviation, right bundle branch block and right ventricular hypertrophy.

31. DUCTUS ARTERIOSUS   BE

The ductus arteriosus joins the pulmonary artery and the aorta and in the foetus allows oxygenated blood from the right ventricle to bypass the lungs. Within 24 hours of birth the ductus closes in response to the increased oxygen concentration of arterial blood. Patent ductus arteriosus occurs three times more commonly in females than males and there is an increased incidence in infants born at high altitude. Patent ductus arteriosus accounts for approximately 15% of all congenital heart disease.

Clinical features of an uncomplicated ductus include: collapsing pulse, left ventricular hypertrophy and a continuous machinery murmur with systolic accentuation which may be heard at the second left intercostal space, beneath the left clavicle and posteriorly over the scapula. The murmur is often only heard in late systole and early diastole.

Recognized complications include: infective endocarditis, heart failure and Eisenmenger's syndrome.

Indomethacin has been used with some success in promoting closure (mechanism − inhibition of prostaglandin E), otherwise surgical ligation is recommended before 2 years of age. The development of an Eisenmenger's syndrome is a contraindication to surgery.

Due to the risk of endocarditis, an antibiotic prophylactic is recommended for dental treatment.

The differential diagnosis of a collapsing pulse includes
    Aortic incompetence
    Patent ductus arteriosus
    Thyrotoxicosis
    Fever/Sepsis
    Pregnancy
    High output cardiac failure e.g. Paget's disease, anaemia

The differential diagnosis of a continuous murmur includes
    Patent ductus arteriosus
    Mitral incompetence and aortic incompetence
    Ventricular septal defect and aortic incompetence

32. GIANT CELL ARTERITIS   BCDE

Giant cell arteritis is a large vessel granulomatous vasculitis which typically occurs in those over the age of 60 years, females are affected more commonly than males. Arteries in the region of the carotid artery are primarily affected.

Clinical features include weight loss, myalgia, arthralgia, fever, headaches, scalp tenderness, tender temporal arteries, pulseless temporal arteries and jaw claudication.

Recognized complications of untreated giant cell arteritis include myocardial infarction, blindness (up to 30% of untreated patients) and stroke.

The disease has many features in common with polymyalgia rheumatica and the two disorders form a spectrum of disease. The diagnosis is usually made on the basis of the history, clinical examination and the demonstration of an elevated ESR and/or CRP. The diagnosis should always be confirmed by performing a temporal artery biopsy; the vasculitic process is however patchy and it is not always possible to demonstrate the characteristic fragmentation of the internal elastic lamina with associated cell infiltrate, granulomata and areas of necrosis.

The diagnosis is a medical emergency and treatment with prednisolone 60 mg per day should be commenced immediately (Note: the biopsy may be usefully performed 24-48 hours after commencing treatment). The dose of corticosteroids may gradually be reduced over a period of months according to the clinical state and acute phase response.

Giant cell arteritis may be paraneoplastic in origin. Failure of clinical symptoms to respond to corticosteroids should alert the physician to this possibility.

33. HODGKIN'S DISEASE   BCE

Hodgkin's disease is commoner in men than women. There are two age peaks at 15-22 and 55-75 years of age.
The disease is characterized by the presence of Reed-Sternberg cells

The disease is characterized by the presence of Reed-Sternberg cells and four histological variants are described:
   Lymphocyte predominant (10-15%), which has the best prognosis
   Lymphocyte depleted (5-15%)
   Mixed cellularity (20-40%)
   Nodular sclerosing (20-50%)

Patients present with enlarged lymph nodes or with constitutional symptoms (B symptoms) of pruritus, fever, alcohol induced pain in affected sites, and > 10% weight loss.

The disease is staged according to the Ann Arbor classification
Stage I-A single lymph node or extralymphatic site
Stage II-Two or more lymph node regions or an extranodal site and
            lymph nodes on the same side of the diaphragm
Stage III-Nodes on both sides of the diaphragm with or without splenic
            enlargement
Stage IV-Diffuse enlargement of one or more extralymphatic sites,
            with or without lymphadenopathy.

Good prognostic factors are youth, lymphocyte predominant histology and the absence of B symptoms. In general, stages I and II are treated with radiotherapy and stages III and IV with chemotherapy.

Note: Alcohol induced pain in affected sites is a recognized feature. If patients have mediastinal lymphadenopathy they may experience chest pain.

34. BITEMPORAL HEMIANOPIA   B

Bitemporal hemianopia results from compression of the optic chiasma e.g. due to pituitary macroadenomas with suprasellar extension.
Acromegaly is frequently caused by acidophil macroadenomas. Occipital lobe lesions are associated with a homonymous hemianopia e.g. a right occipital lobe lesion results in a left homonymous hemianopia (macula sparing is seen in occipital lobe lesions due to posterior cerebral artery occlusion as the macula is represented in the central calcarine sulcus which is supplied by the middle cerebral artery).

35. MUSCLE FASCICULATION   ADE

Fasciculation represents contractions of all motor fibres supplied by one alpha motor neurone and is seen in lower motor neurone lesions (e.g. cervical spondyliasis, syringomyelia, motor neurone disease).

Fibrillation is an EMG finding and represents contraction of individual motor fibres.

36. TRIGEMINAL NEURALGIA   ADE

Trigeminal neuralgia is primarily seen in the elderly; if it occurs in young patients it may be the presenting manifestation of multiple sclerosis. There is a recognized association with trigeminal nerve compression by aberrant vessels in the posterior fossa. The neuralgia is characterized by lancing pain in the distribution of the trigeminal nerve. Pain may be triggered by a variety of stimuli including cold wind and brushing the hair. Symptoms may deteriorate with age. Carbamazepine and phenytoin are effective in relieving symptoms. Surgical section of the nerve or phenol injection are reserved for resistant cases.

37. INTRACRANIAL BERRY ANEURYSMS   CE

Berry aneurysms are found on the anterior communicating cerebral artery in 30% of cases, the middle cerebral artery in 25% of cases and the posterior communicating artery in 25% of cases. In 15% of patients multiple berry aneurysms occur. Rupture results in subarachnoid haemorrhage. Clinical features of a subarachnoid haemorrhage include: headache — patients often describe a severe blow to the back of the neck, neck stiffness, nausea, vomiting, photophobia and loss of consciousness with large bleeds. Bruits over the skull are associated with arteriovenous malformations another recognized cause of subarachnoid haemorrhage. All cases of suspected subarachnoid haemorrhage should be investigated, in the first instance with a head CT scan. Lumbar puncture confirms the diagnosis. CSF shows uniform blood staining, xanthochromia and high protein; the glucose level may be low as the red blood cells utilize sugar.

Arteriography to determine the site of haemorrhage should be performed. The timing of this investigation is subject to debate but should be performed before the second week. Surgery to clip the aneurysm and prevent further bleeding should be performed where possible.

One third of patients die during the first subarachnoid haemorrhage, one third have a second bleed between the first and second week and of these one third survive.

38. PARASUICIDE   BCDE

Parasuicide or attempted suicide due to drug overdose is the commonest cause of acute female medical admissions and in males is second only to acute myocardial ischaemia.

Parasuicide or attempted suicide is commonest in young adults. Risk factors include: low social class, unstable relationships, unemployment and chronic medical illness e.g. epilepsy. Serious psychiatric illness (usually depressive) is present in less than 10% of cases.

The following factors are associated with an increased suicide risk after an attempted suicide
   i)   male, over 45 years of age
   ii)   unemployed
   iii) alcoholism
   iv)   socially isolated
   v)   a history of physical or mental illness
   vi)   patients who experience a profound sense of hoplessness regarding their future
   vii) previous suicide attempts
   viii) writing a suicide note

39. ANOREXIA NERVOSA   AB

Anorexia nervosa is commoner in females and has a peak incidence of 13-14 years of age. Anorexics are obsessed with food. At meal times they pick at food and eat little, and often leave the table early to vomit in private. Loss of 25% of original body weight and failure to maintain body weight above the minimum for height and age are used as diagnostic criteria for anorexia nervosa. Anorexics often exercise daily in a bid to help weight loss. Clinical features include: excess fine lanugo hair, absent or scant axillary and pubic hair, amenorrhoea, hypotension, oedema and bradycardia.

40. **INTELLECTUAL DETERIORATION**   **ABCD**

In clinical practice common reversible causes of intellectual deterioration include subdural haemorrhage, hypothyroidism and B_{12} deficiency.

Huntington's chorea is an autosomal dominant disorder which usually manifests between the ages of 30-50 years. Clinical features include chorea and intellectual deterioration leading to pre-senile dementia. Tetrabenazine is used to treat the chorea. Death after 10-15 years is usual.

Insulinoma, a tumour of pancreatic islet cells is one of the commonest recognized cause of fasting induced hypoglycaemia. 10% of tumours are malignant. Prolonged hypoglycaemic episodes are associated with irreversible cerebral damage — the temporal lobes are primarily affected and temporal lobe lesions may be detected by MRI scanning.

General paresis of the insane is a late complication of systemic syphilis. Cortical degeneration results in widened sulci and dilated ventricles, the dorsal columns degenerate and the meninges are thickened. Clinical features include: intellectual deterioration, epilepsy, euphoria, ataxia, Argyll Robertson pupils and upper motor neurone signs. The Fluorescent Treponeal Antibody Absorption Test (FTAA) and Treponema pallidum Haemagglutination test (TPHA) are positive in >95% of cases.

Thiamine deficiency is a common consequence of chronic alcoholism and may lead to either a Wernicke's encephalopathy or a Korsakoff's psychosis. The later is associated with loss of short term memory and confabulation.

41. PSYCHOGENIC SYMPTOMS   **ABCD**

Common psychogenic symptoms include exhaustion, erectile impotence, left inframammary pain and inability to take a deep enough breath.

Seeing coloured haloes around lights is a common symptom of migrainous headaches.

42. CATARACTS   **ACE**

Cataracts occur in response to a wide range of physical, chemical or mechanical insults to the eye.

Causes of cataracts include:
Congenital
   Galactosaemia
   Dystrophia myotonica
   Hepatolenticular degeneration
   Down's syndrome
   Hurler's syndrome
   Refsum's disease
   Laurence-Moon-Biedl syndrome
   Rubella
   Cretinism

Acquired
   Secondary to ocular disease, e.g. chronic uveitis, retinal detachment, myopia
   Diabetes mellitus
   Hypoparathyroidism
   Ionizing, infrared and microwave radiation
   Drugs e.g. chronic use of corticosteroids and phenothiazines
   Senility

Sarcoidosis and Crohn's disease are both associated with anterior uveitis.

25% of patients with sarcoidosis have ocular involvement at some stage. Ocular manifestations include band keratopathy, glaucoma, uveitis, retinal vasculitis, candle wax exudates (areas of focal periphlebitis), cataracts and localised granulomatous lesions which can occur in the choroid, retina, optic disc, conjunctiva and lacrimal duct.

Note: Many ophthalmologists recognize that cataracts are a long term complication of sarcoidosis.

43. PLEURAL EFFUSION   ABC

Pleural effusions may be divided into exudates (protein concentration > 30 g/l) and transudates (protein concentration > 30 g/l.)

Common causes of pleural transudates include
    Cardiac failure
    Nephrotic syndrome
    Liver failure

Other causes of pleural transudates are
    Meig's syndrome — ovarian fibromas
    constrictive pericarditis
    peritoneal dialysis fluid

Common causes of pleural exudates include
    Pneumonia e.g. streptococcal pneumonia
    Tuberculosis
    Bronchial carcinoma
    Mesothelioma
    Pulmonary infarction
    Rheumatoid arthritis
    SLE
    Subphrenic abscess
    Lymphoma
    Dressler's syndrome
    Yellow nail syndrome

44. EXTRINSIC ALLERGIC ALVEOLITIS   BCE

Extrinsic allergic alveolitis is a hypersensitivity pneumonitis to organic dusts. The antigens include avian droppings, mouldy hay

(*Micropolyspora faeni*) and mouldy sugar cane. The acute form is characterized by cough, fever, shortness of breath and myalgia within a short time of exposure to the relevant antigen. Wheeze is not a feature as there is no airway obstruction. Examination reveals basal crackles. Recovery is usually rapid when the patient is not exposed to the antigen e.g. an individual exposed to the antigen at work may be symptomatic in the evening but have recovered by the following morning.

Continuous low dose exposure to antigen may result in chronic extrinsic allergic alveolitis, characterized by progressive shortness of breath. After repeated attacks lung fibrosis occurs which if allowed to progress will lead to cor pulmonale. Radiologically the severe acute form may be associated with a mid and basal zone alveolar infiltrate and the chronic form of extrinsic allergic alveolitis is associated with predominant upper lobe fibrosis. Pulmonary function shows a pure restrictive defect. Precipitating antibodies are rarely identified unless the case involves avian antigen.

A combination of type III and type IV hypersensitivity is thought to underlie the disease. Peripheral eosinophilia is rare.

Recognized causes of eosinophilia include
Parasitic diseases e.g. hookworm , amoebiasis, ascariasis, filariasis etc.
Allergic disorders e.g. asthma, hay fever, urticaria
Dermatoses e.g. eczema, dermatitis herpetiformis
Drug hypersensitivity
Pulmonary eosinophilia
Churg-Strauss syndrome
Hodgkin's disease
Recovery from acute infection

45. ACUTE BRONCHIOLITIS   ACE

Acute bronchiolitis is the commonest severe acute respiratory tract infection seen in infants and preschool children. Respiratory syncytial virus is responsible for the majority of cases, other organisms implicated include influenza, para-influenza, rhino- and adeno-viruses.

The terminal bronchioles (75-300 μm diameter) are primarily involved in the inflammatory process and luminal obstruction occurs secondary to oedema, cell debris and inspissated secretions. Clinical features are of cough, fever and shortness of breath. Severe cases progress to cyanosis and clinical signs include tachycardia, a barrel shaped hyperexpanded chest with widespread inspiratory crepitations and expiratory rhonchi. Chest X-ray confirms a hyperexpanded chest with areas of segmental collapse. If the child is moderately distressed admission should be arranged and the child monitored for episodes of apnoea and bradycardia. Management is supportive with humidified oxygen; antibiotics are withheld unless there is evidence of secondary bacterial infection. Corticosteroids are not beneficial and neither is physiotherapy in the acute stage. Severe cases may require a period of intermittent ventilation.

46. BRONCHIAL ADENOMA   CD

Bronchial adenomas are slow growing intrabronchial lesions which are usually found in the major bronchi. Bronchial adenomas have now been sub classified into 3 groups
  i)   bronchial carcinoids
  ii) muco-epidermoid tumours
  iii) adenoid cystic tumours
These tumours are capable of local infiltration and metastatic spread; they are not associated with cigarette smoking.

Presenting features include cough, haemoptysis and recurrent chest infection. In addition carcinoids may present with flushing, wheeze, diarrhoea and abdominal pain.

Chest X-ray may show a single nodule or segmental/lobar collapse. Bronchoscopy and biopsy is often complicated by haemorrhage. Adenomas should be treated by resection; the prognosis is good provided metastatic spread has not occurred.

47. ULCERATIVE COLITIS   BCD

Local complications of ulcerative colitis include
  Colonic perforation

Toxic megacolon
Haemorrhage
Colonic carcinoma

More rarely (and commoner in Crohn's disease)
    abscess — ischiorectal
    fistulae-rectovaginal, fistula in ano
    strictures

Distant associations/complications of ulcerative colitis
Skin and mucous membranes
    apthous ulcers
    pyoderma gangrenosum
    erythema nodosum
    erythema multiforme
Ocular
    episcleritis
    uveitis
Musculoskeletal
    oligoarthritis — seronegative
    sacroiliitis
Hepatic
    reversible fatty change — with severe attacks of colitis
    pericholangitis
    chronic active hepatitis
    cirrhosis
    sclerosing cholangitis
    cholangiocarcinoma

48. HEPATOLENTICULAR DEGENERATION (WILSON'S DISEASE)   ACDE

Wilson's disease is an autosomal recessive disorder affecting copper metabolism, characterized by low serum caeruloplasmin (copper binding protein), low or normal serum copper levels and increased urinary copper excretion. In the absence of caeruloplasmin, copper is loosely bound to albumin and tissue copper deposition results; the tissues most commonly affected are the liver, basal ganglia and the kidneys.

The age of presentation varies widely from 5 to 50 years. The younger patients tend to present with hepatic damage and the older patients with neurological signs.

Clinical features include: jaundice, cirrhosis, hepatosplenomegaly, chorea-athetosis, dysarthria, ataxia, dementia, proximal renal tubule acidosis, osteoporosis, arthralgia, haemolytic anaemia, fever and corneal Kayser-Fleisher rings (copper deposition in Descemet's membrane — densest at the superior limbus).

Patients should be treated by restriction of dietary copper and urine copper excretion can be increased with penicillamine.

49. COELIAC DISEASE ABCD

Coeliac disease is associated with the haplotype A1 B8 DR3. The aetiology is unknown but the disease is characterized by hypersensitivity to gliadin a component of gluten which is found in wheat, barley, rye and oats.

The incidence in the UK is of the order of 1: 2,000 and this rises to 1: 300 in Western Ireland.

Coeliac disease may present in infancy at the time of weaning or adulthood and may follow an infection, pregnancy or gastrectomy. Clinical features include: malabsorption, weight loss, failure to thrive, diarrhoea, aphthous ulceration, hyposplenism, clubbing, hypo-or hyper-pigmentation.

Investigations may reveal anaemia (iron deficiency or megaloblastic due to folic acid deficiency, B_{12} deficiency is rare), hypo-albuminaemia, osteomalacia. Small bowel biopsy (jejunum/duodenum-jejunal flexure) characteristically shows subtotal villous atrophy with a chronic inflammatory infiltrate.

The diagnosis is confirmed by placing the patient on a gluten free diet and re-biopsying 8-12 weeeks later to demonstrate normal villous architecture. In children due to the wider differential diagnosis of subtotal villous atrophy many paediatricians will then rechallenge with gluten and re-biopsy.

Long term complications of coeliac disease include an increased risk of small bowel lymphoma and an increased risk of oesophageal carcinoma. There is a well recognized association with other autoimmune diseases.

Note: A rare neurological syndrome characterized by long tract signs and cerebellar ataxia does not respond to gluten withdrawl.

Dermatitis herpetiformis is characterized by a pruritic vesicolo-bullous rash. Histologically IgA is deposited in the dermis. Most patients are gluten sensitive and have evidence of subtotal villous atrophy. The rash will often respond to a gluten free diet. Dapsone is used for resistant cases.

The differential diagnosis of subtotal villous atrophy includes
Coeliac disease
Tropical sprue
Giardiasis
Rota virus infection
Cow's milk protein intolerance
Whipple's disease

50. DUODENAL ULCER   ABCE

A duodenal ulcer is a break in the duodenal mucosa usually in the duodenal bulb. The aetiology is multifactorial and contributory factors include
i) Excess acid secretion compared with normals — increased parietal cell mass, increased stimulation of parietal cells and increased parietal cell sensitivity to secretagogues and stimulants all contribute. Patients have high nocturnal unstimulated gastric acid outputs
ii) Increased rate of gastric emptying after food ingestion which results in a lower duodenal pH compared with normals
iii) Reduced output of bicarbonate from the duodenal mucosa
iv) An association with *Helicobacter pylori* infection
v) Stress
vi) Incidence in men is greater than in women
vii) Familial tendency

viii) Association with blood group O and with non secretors in saliva of blood group substances

There is no convincing evidence that anti-inflammatory drugs or corticosteroids are associated with an increased incidence of duodenal ulceration.

51. TYPE 1 DIABETES   AB

In the U.K. type I diabetes affects males and females equally and usually appears before 30 years of age with two peaks at 5 years and early adolescence.

Recognized pathogenic factors for insulin dependent diabetes include:

i)   The presence of circulating antibodies directed against the beta islet cells. Over 90% of type 1 diabetics can be shown to have anti-islet cell antibodies within one month of diagnosis. The antibodies then gradually disappear so that only 10% of patients will have detectable antibodies after 20 years. Prospective studies show that they may have a role as a marker for the development of insulin dependent diabetes though they have also been found in non diabetic first degree relatives of patients with type I diabetes.

ii) The HLA antigens B8 DR3 and DR4

iii) Viruses such as coxsackie and mumps have been implicated.

Type II diabetes shows a strong genetic tendency with identical twin studies showing $> 90\%$ concordance compared with $< 60\%$ concordance for type 1 diabetes.

52. ELEVATED PLASMA CORTISOL LEVELS   A

Cortisol binding protein levels increase during pregnancy resulting in elevated plasma levels of cortisol.

Causes of elevated plasma cortisol levels include
Stress
Depression
Alcoholism
Obesity

Pregnancy
Cushing's disease
ACTH secreting tumours
Cortisol secreting adrenal tumours
Iatrogenic e.g. ACTH injections

Congenital adrenal hyperplasia is characterized by low cortisol levels but increased levels of androgens. The commonest enzyme deficiency is 21 hydroxylase deficiency.

Primary hyperaldosteronism (Conn's syndrome) is characterized by high circulating levels of aldosterone.

Patients taking prednisolone will have supressed plasma cortisol levels.

Benzodiazepine use per se is not associated with increased plasma cortisol levels, though depression is a recognized cause of elevated cortisol levels.

53. HYPERTHYROIDISM   ABC

Clinical features of hyperthyroidism include: goitre, weight loss (despite a good or increased appetite), fatiguability, diarrhoea, heat intolerance, sweating, tremor, agitation, lid retraction, cardiac arrhythmias, collapsing pulse, proximal myopathy, peripheral neuropathy, alopecia, chore-athetoid movements, amenorrhoea, hypercalcaemia, onycholysis (Plummer's nails) and occasionally frank psychosis.

Features of Graves's disease include
    Lid lag, exophthalmus, conjunctival oedema, ophthalmoplegia,
      papilloedema and optic atrophy
    Pretibial myxoedema
    Thyroid acropachy (appearance of finger clubbing)

The main clinical features of thyroid crisis are: fever, tachycardias and
    arrhythmias, congestive cardiac failure, agitation, tremor, delirium,
    coma, vomiting, diarrhoea, abdominal pain, jaundice and
    hepatomegaly.

54. ABNORMAL COLOURATION OF URINE ADE

Abnormal colouration of the urine may be due to
Blood, haemoglobin or methaemoglobin — red/brown urine
Bile — brown urine
Homogentisic acid — urine darkens on standing
Porphobilinogen and urobilinogen — urine darkens on standing
Rifampicin — pink urine
Tetracyclines — bright yellow urine
Phenolphthalein derivatives — reddish urine
Methyldopa — dark urine
Iron — black urine
Beetroot — red urine

55. NEPHROTIC SYNDROME BCD

The nephrotic syndrome is defined as proteinuria > 3 g/24 hours which leads to hypoalbuminaemia and dependent oedema.

Recognized associations/complications of the nephrotic syndrome include
i) Hypercholesterolaemia associated with elevated triglyceride levels when the syndrome is severe.
ii) An increased incidence of venous thrombosis — due to loss of antithrombin III and proteins S and C, increased serum fibrinogen levels, and an elevated platelet count. Over-vigorous diuretic therapy may contribute to the thrombotic tendency by causing dehydration and venous stasis.
iii) An increased incidence of pneumococcal peritonitis.
iv) Impaired renal function.

Selective proteinuria i.e. where small molecular weight proteins are lost e.g. albumin while the larger molecular weight globulins are retained is a feature of minimal change glomerulonephritis. Non-selective proteinuria is a feature of membranous and proliferative glomerulonephritis.

Spontaneous remissions are most commonly seen in cases of minimal change but can occur with most of the recognized causes of nephrotic syndrome.

Minimal change glomerulonephritis has a peak age in children 1-5 years of age and accounts for >90% of cases of nephrotic syndrome in this age group. Corticosteroid therapy will induce a remission in over 90% of children within 4-6 weeks. Relapse rates may approach 60% and 30% of children become steroid dependent.

Recognized causes of the nephrotic syndrome include
Primary glomerulonephritis
  Minimal change glomerulonephritis
  Membranous glomerulonephritis
  Focal segmental glomerulosclerosis
  Mesangiocapillary (membranoproliferative)
Systemic disease
  Systemic lupus erythematosus
  Primary systemic vasculitis e.g. Henoch-Schönlein purpura
  Amyloidosis
  Diabetes mellitus
Drugs and toxins
  Gold
  Penicillamine
  Mercury
Malignancy
  Carcinoma
  Lymphoma
Pregnancy
  Pre-eclampsia/eclampsia
Congenital
  Finnish nephrotic syndrome
  Diffuse mesangial sclerosis

56. ACUTE TUBULAR NECROSIS   **BE**

Differentiation of oliguric pre-renal failure from acute tubular necrosis

Pre-renal failure
  Pre-renal failure is characterized by the production of small
  volumes of concentrated urine
  Urine sodium <20 mmol/l
  Urine urea >250 mmol/l

Urine osmolality > 500 mosmol/kg
Urine/plasma osmolality > 1.5
Urine/plasma urea > 20
Urine microscopy normal
Note: The kidneys are able to retain sodium.

Acute tubular necrosis

Urine sodium > 20 mmol/l
Urine urea < 150 mmol/l
Urine osmolality > 350 mosmol/kg
Urine/plasma osmolality < 1.1
Urine /plasma urea < 10
Urine microscopy sediment − granular casts, tubular cells
Note: The kidneys are unable to retain sodium or concentrate urea.

Causes of an elevated plasma urea and normal plasma creatinine

Gastrointestinal haemorrhage
Corticosteroid therapy
Tetracycline therapy
Low glomerular filtration rate/dehydration
Excess protein intake

Causes of papilloedema include

Raised intracranial pressure
Accelerated phase hypertension
Retinal vein thrombosis
Papillitis
Carbon dioxide retention
Hypoparathyroidism
Exophthalmos
Lead poisoning
Vitamin A toxicity

57. CHILDHOOD OBESITY   DE

Obesity is common in affluent countries but is not linked to social class. The majority of childhood cases are of simple obesity and these individuals are usually taller than their peers. Approximately 70% of obese children have one or more obese parents, usually the mother suggesting a genetic tendency. Obese children are more likely than their peers to develop into obese adults.

There are a number of congenital syndromes associated with obesity but these are a minority and include

Prader-Willi syndrome frequency 1:2,000
Translocation involving chromosome 15
Clinical features: hyperphagia, obesity, hypogonadism, polydactyly, short stature and hypotonia

Alström syndrome
Autosomal recessive
Clinical features: obesity, hypogonadism, polydactyly, retinal degeneration, deafness and diabetes mellitus.

Lawrence-Moon and Bardet-Biedl syndromes
Autosomal recessive
Clinical features include: obesity, low I.Q., retinitis pigmentosa, hypogonadism (usually secondary) and polydactyly.

Other inherited causes of obesity associated with hypogonadism include Edward's syndrome and the Vasquez syndrome.

The rare Morgani-Stewart-Morel syndrome usually manifests in adult females with obesity, virilism, hyperostosis, poor memory and epilepsy.

58. DOWN'S SYNDROME   BCE

Down's syndrome (trisomy 21) usually arises from non-disjunction of chromosomes 21 at meiosis in the formation of the ovum. The risk rises from approximately 1:1,000 for women 20-29 years of age to 1:60 for women 40-45 years of age. A couple with one Down's child due to non dysjunction run an overall risk of 1:100 of having a second Down's baby. Approximately 6% arise by Robertsonian translocation usually involving chromosomes 14 and 21. A woman carrying such a translocation has a 1 : 8 risk of a Down's baby and a father a 1:50 chance. 2% of cases are associated with chromosomal mosaicism which arises by mitotic non-dysjunction after formation of the zygote. Mongol mosaics may have a normal I.Q. but tend to bear the physical stigmata of the syndrome, the greater number of cells carrying the trisomy the greater the abnormality. As the majority of women giving birth are between the ages of 20-29 years it follows that most Down's babies are born to 20-29 year old mothers.

Clinical features of Down's syndrome include: oval face with prominent epicanthic folds, large tongue, brachycephaly, mental retardation, general hypotonia, short stature, Brushfield spots, transverse palmar crease, dermatoglyphic abnormalities, incurving little fingers, strabismus and nystagmus. 40% of patients have cardiovascular abnormalities which include atrial septal defect, ventricular septal defect, Fallot's tetralogy and patent ductus arteriosus. Other recognized associations include duodenal atresia, imperforate anus, hypothyroidism, cataracts and male infertility. A decline in I.Q. in late childhood is often associated with the development of intracerebral pathological changes consistent with Alzheimer's disease. The incidence of leukaemia in Down's syndrome is 10-18 times that in the normal population.

59. ACUTE GASTROENTERITIS IN CHILDHOOD   BDE

Causes of acute gastroenteritis in childhood in the U.K. include
Bacteria such as *Salmonellae, Shigellae, E. coli, Campylobacter* and *Staphylococcus aureus*.

Viruses such as rotavirus, Norwalk-like viruses, adenoviruses, coronaviruses and togaviruses.

More rarely: *Giardia lamblia, Cryptosporidium, Entamoeba histolytica*.

Rotaviruses are responsible overall for approximately 60% of childhood cases of gastroenteritis. Epidemics occur in the winter, children between 6-24 months are primarily affected.

Dehydration from gastroenteritis is a common cause of death in the third world and in the U.K. is the fifth commonest cause of death in children less than 1 year. The degree of dehydration may be assessed clinically but a recent reliable weight is the best guide to fluid loss. 5% dehydration is associated with loss of skin turgor, depressed fontanelles, sunken eyes, mild lethargy and normal peripheral pulses. 10% dehydration is associated with mottled skin with poor capillary return, tachycardia, small volume pulse, prostration and deeply depressed fontanelles and eyes.

The majority of cases of acute gastroenteritis can be treated with clear fluids (standardized electrolyte solutions e.g. Dioralyte) and breast fed babies may continue to have breast milk during the acute illness. Moderate to severe dehydration (5% dehydration) is an indication for hospitalization and measurement of serum electrolytes to assess whether dehydration is isotonic or hypertonic.

Antibiotics are not indicated unless systemic bacterial infection has occurred; antidiarrhoeal agents are contraindicated as they encourage persistence of pathogenic organisms.

Post gastroenteritis diarrhoea is common and may be due to lactose intolerance, secondary cow's milk protein intolerance or secondary bacterial overgrowth.

60. SYSTOLIC MURMUR IN THE NEWBORN DE

The incidence of congenital heart disease is of the order 7-12 per 1,000. No aetiological factors can be identified in the majority of cases. Genetic abnormalities associated with congenital heart disease include:

Down's syndrome (see above)

Turner's syndrome − XO − coarctation of the aorta (associated with absent foot pulses)

Cri du Chat − partial deletion of chromosome 5 − ventricular septal defect (VSD)

Patau's syndrome − trisomy 13 or 15 − VSD, patent ductus arteriosus and dextrocardia

Edward's syndrome − trisomy 18 − atrial septal defect (ASD), VSD, and Fallot's tetralogy)

Marfan's syndrome − autosomal dominant − aortic regurgitation, mitral valve prolapse

Intrauterine infections such as rubella and drugs such as thalidomide are also associated with congenital heart disease.

Ten to fifteen percent of children with congenital heart disease have an associated non cardiac abnormality involving the gastrointestinal system (e.g. imperforate anus) skeletal system or urogenital syndrome.

JUNE 1990

1.   CUTANEOUS MARKERS OF SYSTEMIC DISEASE   BC

Necrobiosis lipoidica is one of the dermatological associations of
diabetes mellitus. Classically, the appearance is of a well defined
yellow infiltrated plaque with telangiectatic vessels over the edge.

Other cutaneous features of diabetes include: diabetic dermopathy,
bacterial infections (folliculitis, boils, carbuncles etc), candidiasis,
neuropathic ulcers, eruptive xanthomata and ischaemic skin changes.

Vitiligo is recognized as the cutaneous marker of autoimmune disease.
Overall, vitiligo affects 1% of the population and it is associated with
the presence of antimelanocyte antibodies. The areas of depigmentation are usually symmetrical but asymmetrical lesions
following dermatomes can occur.

Conditions associated with vitiligo include
     Thyroiditis — Graves's and Hashimoto's
     Addison's disease
     Pernicious anaemia
     Diabetes mellitus
     Premature ovarian failure
     Hypoparathyroidism
     Fibrosing alveolitis
     Renal tubular acidosis
     Chronic active hepatitis
     Systemic sclerosis
     Morphoea

Alopecia areata, premature greying and halo naevi are also associated
with autoimmune disease.

Pityriasis rosacea is a rash of unknown aetiology. A herald patch on
the trunk precedes the eruption of numerous small satellite lesions over
the trunk. These erythematous lesions have a classical collarette of
scales around the edge. Pruritus may be a problem. The natural

history is resolution over a 6-8 week period.

Pompholyx is one of the types of atopic eczema characterized by vesicular lesions over the palms and soles.

The plant *Primula obconica* is a recognized cause of dermatitis.

2.   PAROTID SWELLING   ABCDE

The differential diagnosis of parotid swelling includes
Infection — viral e.g. mumps
                    bacterial (debilitation)
Sialolithiasis
Sarcoidosis
Sjögren's syndrome
Alcoholic cirrhosis
Lymphoma
Parotid tumour
Diabetes
Amyloidosis
Hyperlipidaemia

3.   CHILDHOOD HYPOKALAEMIC ALKALOSIS   B

Hypokalaemic alkalosis is a recognized finding in pyloric stenosis.

Pyloric stenosis usually presents in the first born male child at four to six weeks. The inheritance is multifactorial. Hypertrophy and hyperplasia of the pylorus results in projectile vomiting soon after feeding. The diagnosis is made clinically: the hypertrophied pylorus may be felt and visible stomach peristalsis may be present. Surgical intervention (Ramstedt's procedure) is indicated once the electrolyte imbalance has been corrected.

The metabolic abnormality associated with ureteric implantation into the sigmoid colon is a hyperchloraemic metabolic acidosis. The other causes of a normal anion gap metabolic acidosis i.e. a hyperchloraemic acidosis) are acetazolamide therapy, renal tubular acidosis and loss of bicarbonate from a pancreatic or biliary fistula.

Hypernatraemia is a recognized consequence of feeding a baby powdered milk that is too concentrated.

Note: Compared with human milk, cow's milk has a higher concentration of protein, sodium, fat and phosphorus.

4. **X-LINKED RECESSIVE DISEASES**   **BCD**

X-linked recessive conditions characteristically manifest in males and are transmitted by females. It is possible for females to exhibit disease manifestations if they are unlucky enough to inherit two affected X chromosomes. More commonly, symptoms may arise if a large percent of the normal X chromosomes are inactivated leaving a predominance of affected X chromosomes e.g. 'Lyonisation' may cause mild haemophilia in female carriers. Sons of affected fathers will be unaffected as they inherit the Y chromosome. All daughters of affected fathers will be carriers. 50% of daughters of carrier mothers will be carriers and 50% of sons will be affected.

X-linked recessive conditions include
Colour blindness
Haemophilia A and B
Glucose 6 phosphate dehydrogenase deficiency
Congenital sideroblastic anaemia
Lesch-Nyhan syndrome
Fabry's disease
Alport's syndrome
Ocular albinism
Duchenne muscular dystrophy
Hunter's syndrome
Nephrogenic diabetes insipidus
Chronic granulomatous disease
Lowe's syndrome
Pseudohypoparathyroidism

Vitamin D resistant rickets (hypophosphataemic) is an X-linked dominant trait.

5. **SIXTH CRANIAL (ABDUCENT) NERVE**   **AD**

The sixth cranial nerve (abducent nerve) supplies the lateral rectus muscle. Its nucleus is situated in the lower pons and the nerve leaves the inferior border of the pons near the midline to pass through the posterior and middle cranial fossae, the cavernous sinus where it runs lateral to the internal carotid artery and the superior orbital fissure to reach the lateral rectus. Its long intracranial course renders it susceptible to damage by all causes of raised intracranial pressure — a false localizing sign. A sixth nerve palsy results in diplopia and a convergent squint.

6. **CEREBRAL CORTICAL LESIONS**   **ABE**

The déjà-vu phenomenon is a feature of temporal lobe epilepsy.

Occipital lobe tumours are a recognized cause of homonymous hemianopias.

Frontal lobe lesions are associated with abnormal social behaviour, incontinence, poor memory, intellectual impairment and a contralateral grasp and palmomental reflex.

Jacksonian seizures are a recognized feature of lesions of the precentral gyrus.

Parietal lobe lesions are associated with dyscalculi, dysgraphia, dyslexia, finger agnosia, left-right disorientation and asterognosis. Non-dominant parietal lobe lesions are specifically associated with sensory inattention and dressing apraxia.

A motor or expressive dysphasia involves the dominant inferior frontal gyrus — Broca's area.

A sensory or receptive dysphasia involves the posterior part of the dominant superior temporal gyrus — Wernicke's area.

A pure nominal dysphasia results from a lesion in the posterior part of the dominant superior temporal gyrus and adjacent inferior parietal lobule.

Global dysphasia (combined motor and sensory dysphasia) results from left middle cerebral artery infarction and involves both the Broca and Wernicke areas.

7. NEUROTRANSMITTERS SYNTHESIS BE

Dopa decarboxylase is involved in the synthesis of noradrenaline.

Glutamic acid decarboxylase is involved in the synthesis of gamma-aminobutyric acid.

Acetylcholine is metabolized by cholinesterase and pseudo-cholinesterase.

Catechol-O methyl transferase and monoamine oxidase are involved in the metabolism of adrenaline and noradrenaline. Monoamine oxidase is also involved in the metabolism of serotonin (5-hydroxytryptamine).

8. RENAL TUBULE PHYSIOLOGY BCD

70% of sodium, bicarbonate and water is reabsorbed in the proximal convoluted tubule. Amino acids, glucose, phosphate and urate are also reabsorbed by the proximal tubule cells.

The loop of Henle, by means of the countercurrent multiplier system, creates an osmotic gradient in the medulla. The amount of water then reabsorbed is dependent on circulating levels of anti-diuretic hormone and the responsiveness of the distal convoluted tubule and collecting duct to anti-diuretic hormone.

Renin is secreted by the juxtaglomerular apparatus in response to a low sodium concentration in the distal convoluted tubule. Renin via stimulation of angiotensin I and angiotensin II leads to aldosterone secretion. Aldosterone acts on the distal convoluted tubule to promote sodium reabsorption — each sodium ion reabsorbed is exchanged for either one hydrogen or one potassium ion.

Extracellular fluid depletion leads to increased aldosterone secretion which leads to a net loss of potassium ions. In the presence of a systemic alkalosis hydrogen ions are preserved and potassium ions are preferentially exchanged for sodium resulting in hypokalaemia.

9. FAMILIAL (TYPE IIA) HYPERCHOLESTEROLAEMIA   ABCD

Type IIa or familial hypercholesterolaemia (autosomal dominant inheritance) is characterized by high levels of low density lipoproteins (LDL levels). There is a deficiency of LDL receptors. Early onset ischaemic heart disease is the commonest mode of presentation in heterozygotes and the average age span for untreated homozygotes is 20 years. Other clinical features in heterozygotes include tendon xanthomas (achilles, extensor tendons of hands), xanthelasmata, corneal arcus and a polyarthritis. In addition, homozygotes have cutaneous xanthomas and may develop supravalvular aortic stenosis. Note: Low density lipoproteins are composed primarily of cholesterol. LDL is the end product after triglycerides have been removed from VLDL.

10. ELEVATED SERUM PARATHYROID HORMONE LEVELS   AC

Chronic renal failure is a common cause of secondary and tertiary hyperparathyroidism.

Hypercalcaemia and a normal alkaline phosphate level are features of multiple myeloma; parathyroid hormone levels are repressed. Alkaline phosphatase levels are elevated in the presence of pathogenic fracture.

A raised alkaline phosphatase and normal serum calcium and phosphate are the usual findings in Paget's disease, though immobilization may be associated with hypercalcaemia.

Pseudohypoparathyroidism is an X-linked inherited disease characterized by end organ resistance to PTH. Clinical features include short stature, a round face, short metacarpals and metatarsal bones, and low I.Q. Serum biochemistry shows hypocalcaemia, hyperphosphataemia, an elevated PTH level and normal serum creatinine and vitamin D levels.

11. ASPIRIN TOXICITY   BD

Clinical features of aspirin toxicity include: nausea, vomiting, epigastric pain, sweating, hyperpyrexia, irritability, tinnitus, increased respiratory rate; (pulmonary oedema), dehydration, hypokalaemia and bruising/purpura (due to hypoprothrombinaemia).

Acid base and electrolyte abnormalities of aspirin toxicity
Initially the classical acid base disturbance is a respiratory alkalosis due to direct stimulation of the respiratory centre by salicylates. To compensate for this, bicarbonate is secreted in the urine — with loss of Na, K and water. Later a metabolic acidosis may develop due to a combination of the salicylic acid per se and the salicylate induced inhibition of the TCA cycle which results in an increase in lactate and pyruvate. Stimulation of fat catabolism causes ketone body and β-hydroxybutyrate production (starvation and dehydration contribute) and accelerated protein catabolism causes amino-acidaemia/uria.

Hyperglycaemia or hypoglycaemia are recognized complications. Severe dehydration can result with pre-renal failure.

Salicylate levels of 300-500 mg/l at 6 hours are associated with mild toxicity, levels of 500-750 mg/l with moderate toxicity and >750 mg/l with severe toxicity.

12. SECRETORY IgA   AD

IgA monomer has a molecular weight of 160,000 and is the major immunoglobulin in seromucus secretions e.g. tears, saliva, colostrum, and the gastrointestinal tract. IgA is synthesised by plasma cells in mucosal surfaces and is then dimerised. The dimeric IgA is then complexed with a secretory protein synthesised by local epithelial cells which protects it against proteolysis. IgA prevents micro-organisms from adhering to mucosal cells, it will also activate the alternative (but not classical) complement pathway.

13. MEASLES VACCINE   **ACD**

See February 1990 question 15.

14. INFECTIVE CAUSES OF BLOODY DIARRHOEA   **A**

(Bloody diarrhoea is not a feature of giardiasis or cholera.)

Shigella sonnei is often associated with a trivial illness, *Shigella flexneri* and *boydi* are of intermediate pathogenicity whereas *Shigella dysenteriae* may be associated with fulminant disease. Shigella has a short incubation period of 2-4 days.

Clinical features of shigella infections include: bloody diarrhoea, abdominal pain, meningism and intussusception in children and reactive arthritis.

The passage of bloody diarrhoea is typical of acute amoebiasis — *Entamoeba histolytica* infection associated with large bowel ulceration. Man is infected with *Entamoeba histolytica* by ingesting cysts excreted by a carrier. In most people the organism survives as an intraluminal commensal. Invasion of the colonic mucosa by trophozoites is favoured by immunosuppression and local colonic disease e.g. carcinoma.

Clinical disease may be divided into
  i)   acute amoebic dysentery,
  ii)   the complications of acute amoebic dysentery — peritonitis, haemorrhage, fistulae and strictures; a right iliac fossa amoebic mass
  iii) hepatic abscess
  iv) complications of hepatic abscess — rupture into chest, pericardium or peritoneum
  v)   cutaneous and genital ulceration.

Approximately 60-80% of patients with large bowel disease will have a positive amoebic fluorescent antibody test compared with over 90% with amoebic hepatic abscess. The finding of large numbers of trophozoites in the stool (not cysts) would confirm the diagnosis of acute colonic amoebiasis.

Chemotherapeutic agents used in the management of amoebiasis include

    metronidazole — acts systemically and on luminal amoebae
    emetine — acts systemically, little luminal activity
    chloroquine — acts solely systemically
    tetracycline — systemically effective
    erythromycin — systemically effective
    diloxanide furoate — acts solely on luminal amoebae

15. PARASITIC INDUCED ANAEMIA   BCD

Taenia saginata infection is usually asymptomatic; recognized clinical symptoms include pruritus ani, nausea and weight loss. Niclosamide is the drug of choice.

Ancylostoma duodenale (hookworm) is the commonest cause of iron deficiency anaemia in the world. Thiabendazole and mebendazole are effective chemotherapeutic agents.

Ascaris lumbricoides infestation is usually asymptomatic. Recognized complications include fever, abdominal pain, intestinal obstruction, cholangitis, hepatic abscess. Loeffler's syndrome is associated with larval migration through the lungs and may lead to pneumonitis and bronchospasm. In children, infection may be associated with failure to thrive. Chemotherapeutic agents include: levamisole, pyrantel pamoate, mebendazole and piperazine salts.

Giardiasis may present with an acute or chronic diarrhoeal illness and is associated with subtotal villous atrophy and malabsorption. Metronidazole is the drug of choice.

Mild chronic blood loss is a recognized feature of *Schistosoma haematobium* though anaemia is unusual if dietary iron is plentiful. At a late stage the anaemia of chronic renal failure may ensue.

16. INSECT VECTORS   ADE

The tsetse fly is responsible for transmisson of African trypanosomiasis (sleeping sickness); melarosopol or suramin are used in the treatment of sleeping sickness.

American trypanosomiasis (Chaga's disease) is transmitted to man by triatomine bugs and may be treated with nifurtinox or benzidazole.

The yellow fever virus is transmitted to man via a mosquito vector (e.g. *Aedes simpsoni* and *A. egypti*). Travellers to endemic areas should be vaccinated with a live attenuated vaccine — immunity is long lasting.

Simulium vectors (black-flies) are involved in the transmission of onchocerciasis to man. Diethylcarbamazepine and suramin have both been successfully used in treatment along with nodulectomy.

Lymphogranuloma venereum is a sexually transmitted disease caused by *Chlamydia trachomata* and should be treated with tetracyclines or sulphonamides.

Schistosomiasis is acquired when part of the body is immersed in fresh water and cercariae (from snails) penetrate the skin. Praziquantel is the drug of choice for all species of schistosomiasis.

17. BLEEDING TIME   BE

The bleeding time is the best single test of platelet function. The bleeding time is prolonged when the platelet count falls below 100 x 10^{12}/l and is also prolonged in cases of functional platelet abnormalities.

Causes of thrombocytopenia
    Decreased platelet production
        bone marrow hypoplasia e.g. drugs
        bone marrow infiltration e.g. leukaemia
        infection e.g. congenital rubella
    Defective platelet maturation
        B_{12} deficiency
    Decreased platelet survival
        idiopathic thrombocytopenia purpura
        splenomegaly
        SLE
        infection
        disseminated intravascular coagulation
        thrombotic thrombocytopenic purpura

haemangiomas

Hereditary disorders of platelet function include
　　Bernard-Soulier syndrome (Aut R) — absent glycoprotein 1b
　　Glanzmann's syndrome (Aut R) — absent glycoproteins 11b-111a
　　Storage pool disease (Aut R or D) — defective release of ADP
　　Grey-platelet syndrome — absent alpha granules
　　Aspirin-like defect — defective release of ADP

Note: Von Willebrand's disease is associated with impaired platelet adhesion and reduced agglutination to ristocetin and is due to deficiency of plasma von Willebrand factor.

The rare genetic disorders Hermansky-Pudlak syndrome, Wiskott-Aldrich syndrome and Chediak-Higashi syndrome are all associated with prolongation of the bleeding time.

18.　SICKLE CELL DISEASE　　　　　　　　　　　　　　DE

Sickle cell disease is an autosomal recessive trait which results from a single amino acid substitution of valine for glutamic acid at the number 6 position in the β chain. The disorder manifests when foetal haemoglobin is replaced by adult haemoglobin.
Clinical features of sickle cell disease include:
a) Anaemia — chronic haemolytic anaemia often associated with a degree of jaundice. The chronic haemolysis may be exacerbated by sickle crises, and four types of sickle crises are recognized

　　i)　thrombotic or vaso-occlusive crises see below
　　ii)　aplastic crises (may be related to infection with parvovirus)
　　iii)　haemolytic crises
　　iv)　sequestration crises (spleen, liver and lung)

Vaso-occlusive crises may result in organ infarction, pain in limbs, abdominal pain, auto-splenectomy, hand-foot syndrome (painful dactylitis of fingers and toes), skin ulceration.

b) Infections — pneumococcus and salmonella
c) Neurological — proliferative retinopathy, hemiplegia, convulsions
d) Renal — haematuria, concentrating defect, nephrotic syndrome

e) Endocrine — delayed puberty

19. BURKITT'S LYMPHOMA   BCE

Burkitt's lymphoma (an undifferentiated lymphoblastic lymphoma) has a peak incidence of 4-7 years and is the commonest childhood neoplasm in equitorial Africa. Large jaw tumours involving the molar and premolar teeth are common; other sites affected include the retroperitoneum, liver, testis, ovary, breast, bone and spinal cord.

Recognized associations include Epstein-Barr virus infection, malarial infection and a chromosomal translocation involving chromosomes 8 and 14.

Characteristically the tumours are chemosensitive, cyclophosphamide has been used with good effect. The prognosis is related to the site and extent of the tumour. Single jaw tumours have an excellent prognosis.

20. ENALAPRIL   ABCD

Enalapril is an angiotensin converting enzyme inhibitor used in the treatment of heart failure and hypertension. Angiotensin converting enzyme breaks down angiotensin I to angiotensin II (primarily in lung endothelium) and also functions in the inactivation of bradykinin. Angiotensin II stimulates aldosterone release and also has a direct vasoconstrictive effect. The inhibition of angiotensin II is believed to be the major therapeutic effect of enalapril though the drug is also effective in decreasing blood pressure in anephric individuals.

Enalapril is a pro-drug absorbed orally and converted into the active enalaprilat by the liver. Enalaprilat has a long half life allowing enalapril to be given once daily. Enalaprilat is excreted by the kidney so the metabolite accumulates in patients with renal impairment.

Recognized side effects include: first dose hypotension, a deterioration in renal function (angiotensin 11 is important in maintaining glomerular efferent arteriolar tone; all patients should have renal function monitored), neutropenia, angioneurotic oedema, rash, and cough.

Note: loss of taste is seen with captopril not enalapril

21. IRON THERAPY AC

Premature infants are liable to develop anaemia early on in life because the blood volume increases rapidly at a time when the marrow remains hypoplastic, iron supplements may be necessary.

Intestinal malabsorption e.g. coeliac disease may present with iron deficient anaemia; co-existent folic acid deficiency is common in these cases.

22. TRICYCLIC ANTIDEPRESSANTS ACD

Recognized side effects of tricyclic antidepressants include
  i)   Autonomic side effects which arise from the anticholinergic action of the drugs coupled with the effect on inhibiting noradrenalinere uptake e.g. hesitancy, loss of accommodation, constipation, postural hypotension, tachycardias, dry mouth, precipitation of glaucoma.
  ii) ECG changes include prolongation of the Q-T interval and flat T waves with ST segment depression. Amitryptiline has been associated with sudden death.
  iii) Tremor, drowsiness and hallucinations.
  iv) Cholestatic jaundice has been described with certain drugs e.g. iprindole.

23. DRUG SIDE EFFECTS ABDE

Drugs commonly associated with peripheral neuropathy include
Nitrofurantoin
Vincristine
Metronidazole
Isoniazid (B6 deficiency)
Ethambutol

Gold
Perhexilene maleate
Amiodarone

Drugs associated with salt and water retention (hypertension/oedema) include
Non steroidal anti-inflammatory agents
Carbenoxalone
Oestrogen contraceptive pill
Minoxidil

Recognized side effects of amiodarone
Photosensitivity
Slate grey colouration of the skin
Corneal microdeposits (reversible)
Hypo/hyperthyroidism
Pulmonary fibrosis
Hepatitis
Peripheral neuropathy

Drugs associated with photosensitivity
Tetracyclines
Amiodarone
Non steroidal anti-inflammatory agents e.g. benoxaprofen
Thiazide diuretics
Frusemide
Chlorpromazine
Chlorpropamide
Sulphonamides
Nalidixic acid

Metoclopramide is a dopamine antagonist which is used as an antiemetic. It acts both centrally on the chemotrigger zone (situated in the floor of the fourth ventricle) and also acts on the stomach, increasing the rate of gastric emptying (by increasing the tone of the oesophageal sphincter and relaxing the pylorus). Extrapyramidal side effects e.g. oculogyric crises arise from dopaminergic blockade.

Co-trimoxazole may unmask folic acid but not B_{12} deficiency.

24. CARBIMAZOLE   ABC

Carbimazole is the drug of choice for the treatment of hyperthyroidism. It inhibits the iodination of tyrosine and inhibits the peroxidase enzyme which releases iodine from iodides. The drug crosses the placenta and is also excreted in the breast milk.

Recognized side effects include agranulocytosis (patients should be warned of this and asked to report immediately any infections whilst on treatment), arthralgia, rashes, jaundice and gastrointestinal upset. Initially the drug is given in a high dose to render the patient euthyroid. The dosage can then often be reduced to a maintenance dose. It is often possible to withdraw the drug after 1-2 years.

Beta blockers are often initially given with carbimazole to control tachycardias and symptoms of anxiety.

25. STATISTICS   AE

$$\text{Variance} = \text{sum} \frac{(x - x)^2}{n-1} = \frac{\text{sum of the squares}}{\text{degrees of freedom}}$$

The standard deviation = square root of the variance.
A p value of 0.001 for the difference between two means is more significant than a value of 0.01. A value of p of 0.001 means that there is a 1:1,000 chance that the difference between the means of two groups occurred by chance. A value of p of 0.01 means that there is a 1:100 chance that the difference between the means of two groups occurred by chance. A p value of 0.05 or less (1:20) is taken as being statistically significant.

26. GIANT CELL ARTERITIS   ABCDE

See February 1990 question 32 for discussion.

Note: Most authorities describe tender pulseless temporal arteries as being characteristic of temporal arteritis.

27. SKELETAL ABNORMALITIES   ACDE

Radiological changes of extramedullary haemopoiesis, such as occurs in thalassaemia major, include thinning of the cortex of overexpanded bones (phalanges, metacarpals, long bones, skull and ribs) with coarsening of remaining trabeculae. Perpendicular striations replace the outer table of the skull resulting in the hair on end appearance.

Radiological changes of sickle cell disease mimic those of thalassaemia. In addition periosteal thickening and the changes of avascular necrosis are common, and the skull X-ray may show a ground glass appearance. Sickle cell dactylitis describes the tender swollen phalanges seen in young children. The underlying pathology is probably a combination of marrow, cortex and periosteal infarction.

Radiological changes of scurvy include
  i) metaphyseal change with a dense band of provisional calcification and a lucent band (deficient ossification) on the diaphyseal side — fractures occur easily in this lucent region resulting in the appearance of lateral spurs
  ii) small epiphyses with a classical thin cortex — Wimburger's sign
  iii) subperiosteal haemorrhages leading to subperiosteal new bone formation (enters the differential diagnosis of non accidental injury).

Skeletal changes in haemophilia include subperosteal haemorrhages which may form large cystic structures — pseudotumours; recurrent haemarthroses may lead to joint destruction — haemophiliac arthropathy.

28. LEFT ATRIAL MYXOMA   ABCDE

Atrial myxomas are the commonest primary cardiac neoplasm. They are more common in females than males. Three-quarters arise from the fossa ovalis and lie in the left atrium; the rest occur in the right atrium apart from the very rare ventricular lesions. The pedunculated tumours are usually benign and recurrence after surgery reflects inadequate removal.

Clinical features include
   i)   evidence of left atrial outflow obstruction — mitral systolic and diastolic murmurs which change with posture, rarely a tumour 'plop' may be heard in early diastole
   ii)   atrial fibrillation
   iii) systemic embolisation often when the patient is in sinus rhythm.
   iv) fever
   v)   clubbing
   vi) elevated ESR and raised immunoglobulins
   vii) normochromic normocytic anaemia
   viii) leucocytosis
   iv) thrombocytosis

29. MITRAL VALVE PROLAPSE   ABCE

Echocardiographic evidence of prolapse of the mitral valve cusps into the left atrium has been reported in approximately 17% of 20 year old females in one large study, the overall incidence in the population being 5%. The typical clinical signs of a mid-systolic click and a late systolic murmur heard at the left sternal edge are less common. The murmur will be exaggerated by factors which decrease cardiac volume, such as performing the Valsalva manoeuvre and the inhalation of amyl nitrate and will be decreased by factors which increase cardiac volume, such as squatting and propranolol.

Most cases are asymptomatic but clinical associations of mitral valve prolapse include:
   i)   infective endocarditis — antibiotic prophylaxis is required for dental and surgical procedures
   ii)   an increased risk of cerebral embolism
   iii) ventricular ectopics
   iv) atypical chest pain — coronary angiography is normal

30. FAT EMBOLISM   BCDE

Fat embolism is a recognized complication of long bone fracture. It complicates approximately 2% of long bone fractures and has a mortality of 10-15%. Fat from the bone marrow enters the circulation soon after the fracture; the clinical symptoms are not however manifest for 2-3 days. It is thought that breakdown of fat emboli and the production of toxic metabolites (e.g. free fatty acids) in small capillaries e.g. in the pulmonary circulation is responsible for tissue damage.

Clinical features include blood-stained sputum, respiratory failure, circulatory failure, confusion and disorientation, a diffuse petechial rash, retinal haemorrhages and thrombocytopenia. Treatment is supportive care in ICU.

31. WOLFF-PARKINSON-WHITE SYNDROME   AC

Wolff-Parkinson-White syndrome (WPW) is the most common re-entry tachycardia. The usual underlying abnormality is an accessory pathway, the Bundle of Kent, bypassing the atrio-ventricular node to the left ventricle (Type A). More rarely the right ventricle is affected (Type B). The characteristic ECG abnormalities are: a short PR interval (< 0.12 s); a wide QRS complex (> 0.1 s); the delta wave — a slurred start to the QRS complex due to early but slow depolarisation through non-specialized myocardium; and left axis deviation. The delta waves are positive in all chest leads in Type A, negative in the right chest leads in Type B, and may only be present intermittently. Interpretation of the ECG is often difficult and WPW may mimic right ventricular hypertrophy, right bundle branch block or a posterior infarct in Type A, and a septal infarct in Type B. A rare variant of WPW has a normal PR interval due to the accessory pathway — Mahaim fibres — connecting the AV node directly to the interventricular septum such that there is pre-excitation but no bypass of the AV node and thus no delta wave.

There are usually no other cardiac abnormalities but WPW is associated with both Ebstein's anomaly and mitral valve prolapse.

Hypertrophic cardiomyopathy may give similar ECG changes to WPW.

The two characteristic paroxysmal arrhythmias associated with WPW are:
  i)   Re-entry tachycardia — this is typically a regular, narrow
       complex tachycardia, unless there is phasic aberrant
       interventricular conduction. It is initiated by a premature

atrial beat which is conducted conventionally via the AV node The accessory pathway repolarises more slowly than the AV node and thus fails to conduct the atrial premature beat. It does, however, conduct retrogradely to the atrium and thus perpetuates the reciprocating tachycardia. The conventional ventricular depolarization eliminates the delta wave during the tachyarrythmia. Treatment is as for other causes of supraventricular tachycardia.

ii) Atrial fibrillation — this is less common but is potentially more serious. Most impulses are via the accessory pathway. This is capable of extremely rapid conduction and the rapid ventricular response may degenerate into ventricular fibrillation. Nodal blocking drugs, digoxin and verapamil, **must** be avoided in this condition as they may accelerate conduction via the accessory pathway. The delta wave is retained and this and the extremely rapid AF allow diagnosis of underlying WPW in these patients so that dangerous therapy may be avoided. Cardioversion is the safest treatment. Amiodarone, quinidine and disopyramide all slow conduction through the accessory pathway. Surgery is occasionally warranted.

Other causes of a short PR interval:
   i) Lown-Ganong-Levine syndrome — the Jame's tract connects the atrium to the lower AV node. There is thus a short PR interval but no delta wave. Re-entry tachycardia may occur and treatment is as for other SVTs.
   ii) Congenitally small AV node
   iii) Sympathetic over activity

32. SPLENECTOMY   **ACDE**

Splenectomy is the definitive treatment for hereditary (autosomal dominant) spherocytosis in all save the most mild cases. The underlying abnormality in the red cell membrane is, of course, unaffected but red cell longevity is effectively normalized and complications such as haemolytic and aplastic crises, folate deficiency and gall stones are avoided. Other types of anaemia which may require splenectomy include: pyruvate kinase deficiency, thalassaemia, and chronic steroid resistant forms of acquired (idiopathic) auto-immune haemolysis. Splenectomy may also be performed for therapeutic reasons in hairy cell leukaemia – for marked splenomegaly or hypersplenism, and chronic lymphocytic leukaemia – for patients with more than stage O or I disease which is non-responsive to other therapy. Splenectomy may be performed in Hodgkin's disease for full staging of clinical I/II disease but has no therapeutic role. Cases of idiopathic thrombocytopenia which do not respond to corticosteroids usually respond to splenectomy.

33. SUBARACHNOID HAEMORRHAGE ABD

Sub-hyaloid haemorrhage is thought to be a consequence of a rapid increase in intracranial pressure at the onset of the subarachnoid haemorrhage (SAH). In severe and prolonged SAH, ophthalmoscopy may also occasionally show papilloedema. The majority of spontaneous (i.e. not related to head injury) SAH are due to a ruptured aneurysm and this is usually within carotid artery territory. Approximately 5% are from arterio-venous malformations and a small number are a consequence of bleeding disorders, tumours or vasculitis. The differential diagnosis of the unconscious patient with glycosuria includes: diabetes; a sub-arachnoid haemorrhage; or an overdose of salicylates. Xanthochromia, due to oxyhaemoglobin from lysed red cells, appears within 2-4 hours of a SAH and only starts to resolve after 7-10 days. Bilirubin is also released from leptomeningeal cells in proportion to the size of the haemorrhage and may give a xanthochromic CSF for a much longer period. Mild xanthochromia, in the absence of sub-arachnoid or intracerebral haemorrhage may occur in association with a high CSF protein (>1 g/l) or severe jaundice.

Vasospasm may affect vessels distant from the bleeding site. It may be suspected clinically in a post-SAH patient whose neurological state deteriorates and in whom further haemorrhage is excluded. It may result in cerebral infarction and is a contraindication to surgery.

34. CHARACTERISTIC FEATURES OF PARKINSON'S DISEASE BC

Parkinson's disease is characterized by a tetrad of rigidity ('lead pipe' or 'cog-wheel'), hypo/bradykinesia, tremor and postural change – any two of these manifestations are required in order to make a clinical diagnosis.

Clinical features include
Paucity of blinking, blepharoclonus and blepharospasm, positive glabellar tap, failure of convergence
Loss of facial expression, expressionless voice, dysphagia
Micrographism
Festinant gait, hand deformities, constipation
Seborrhoea
Urinary frequency and incontinence
Sub-cortical dementia.
The side effects of the drugs used to treat Parkinson's disease must also be considered in the clinical picture.

In the Steele-Richardson-Olszewski syndrome, one of the so-called Parkinsonism Plus disorders, there is also a progressive supranuclear palsy (characteristically affecting upward gaze).

A positive Rhomberg's test indicates Dorsal (posterior) column disease.

The reappearance of primitive reflexes, such as a grasp reflex, pout reflex and the palmo-mental reflex, indicates frontal lobe damage.

35. OPTIC NEURITIS (MULTIPLE SCLEROSIS)   ABCE

A central scotoma is the commonest field defect of acute optic neuritis though other types of scotoma and even homonymous and bitemporal defects may occur according to which part of the optic nerve/chiasm/tract is involved. When papillitis is present, there may also be some enlargement of the blind spot. Clinical features of papillitis include: pain with eye movement and to pressure; variable but often marked visual loss which occurs over a period of 1-3 days and usually recovers completely over a period of 2-4 weeks; and loss of colour and brightness sensation.

Visually evoked potentials are usually elicited using a pattern (checkerboard) reversal or flash stimulus. The vast majority of patients with optic neuritis will have an increased latency, and in only a small proportion of cases does this resolve after resolution of the clinical state. In addition, > 50% of patients with MS who have not had clinical episodes of optic neuritis will also have delayed VEPs. Changes in amplitude of the VEPs are more transient and tend to resolve in parallel with the acute attack.

Macular oedema may occur in diabetic retinopathy, posterior uveitis of whatever cause and venous occlusive disorders. In its early stages it is recognized by blurring of the macular light reflex and may be confirmed by fluorescein angiography. In more serious cases cystic changes develop.

36. LOSS OF VIBRATION SENSE AT BOTH ANKLES   AD

Vibration sense is transmitted via first order neurones in the ipsilateral dorsal (posterior) columns. These synapse in the Gracile and Cuneate nuclei in the medulla with second order neurones which pass via the medial lemniscus to the contralateral thalamus. Third order neurones pass to the sensory cortex (post central gyrus). Vibration sense will be lost in all sensory neuropathies, peripheral nerve lesions and disorders affecting the dorsal (posterior) columns including: subacute combined degeneration of the cords*; tabes dorsalis*; Brown-Sequard syndrome (ipsilateral loss only)*; transverse myelitis; diabetic 'pseudotabes'*; multiple sclerosis; and Friedreich's ataxia *. (* = dissociated sensory loss).

Loss of ankle vibration sense is a normal finding in subjects over 70 years of age.

37. ANOREXIA NERVOSA   B

The typical anorexic is: female (F:M = 20:1); aged 14-17 and has recently been through puberty (though is occasionally pre-pubertal); exercises fanatically; diets obsessively — though has an intense interest in food and over-eating and bullimia may feature; ingests purgatives; has an abnormal body image which may have been reinforced by obesity in youth; may admit to emotional problems and depression and has poor insight into the condition — but is not psychotic. Examination reveals severe wasting, lanugo hair, cold extremities and often a low pulse rate and blood pressure. The endocrine state is characterized by: primary or secondary amenorrhoea; reduced LH and FSH with a pre-pubertal circadian rhythm; an LHRH test gives a disproportionate FSH to LH response; TFTs — normal T4, reduced T3 and increased reverse-T3; normal or increased GH; normal or increased cortisol; reduced oestrogens and increased testosterone; normal prolactin.

38. MOOD DISTURBANCE   ACDE

Emotional lability and incontinence are characteristic features of bilateral cerebrovascular disease.

'Negative' features such as blunting of affect predominate in chronic schizophrenia.

The Korsakov syndrome is almost wholly characterized by loss of short term memory and, compensatory confabulation.

A degree of irritability is common in mania and anxiety is characteristic of delirium tremens.

39. VISUAL HALLUCINATIONS   B

Visual hallucinations are principally a feature of acute organic confusional states, particularly in the elderly, as a result of insults such as:
   Sepsis
   Surgery
   Drug and alcohol intoxication/withdrawal/abuse
   Cerebrovascular events
   Hypoxia
   Vitamin deficiencies
   Metabolic and endocrine disturbances.
   Rarer causes include: hysteria; schizophrenia; severe affective disorders; and complex partial seizures (TLE).

40. MENTAL HANDICAP   ABCD

Tuberose sclerosis (epiloia) is inherited in an autosomal dominant fashion and is characterized by mental retardation, epilepsy, and skin lesions — adenoma sebaceum on the cheeks and forehead, areas of depigmentation on the trunk, subungual fibromas and the 'shagreen patch'. The cerebral lesions often calcify leading to periventricular calcification, cerebral lesions may also undergo malignant transformation.

Other clinical features include retinal phakomas, cardiac rhabdomyosarcomas, pulmonary and renal hamartomas, and renal cysts.

Maternal rubella in the first trimester classically results in the triad of cataracts, heart defects and deafness. Skeletal changes, thrombocytopenia, hepatitis and mental retardation are less common.

Phenylketonuria is an autosomal recessive disorder of aromatic amino acid metabolism and is diagnosed in neonates at 6 days by the demonstration of hyper-phenylalaninaemia in a Guthrie test. Untreated phenylketonuria manifests as: psychomotor delay in early childhood with microcephaly; seizures (Salaam attacks) in $\approx$50% with hypsarrhythmia on EEG in 90%; dilution of skin, hair and iris pigmentation; hyperactivity and bad temper; eczematous skin eruptions; and hyper-reflexia. The excreted urinary aromatic amino acids have a mousy smell. The phenylalanine restricted diet can usually be relaxed after the age of eight.

41. MYCOPLASMA PNEUMONIA   AD

Mycoplasma pneumoniae infection is often preceded by a week of non-specific malaise, fever and headache. Typically one lobe is involved (two lobes in 20%) and pleurisy and effusions are rare. Common extrapulmonary manifestations include: haemolysis due to cold agglutinins (anti-I antibodies) in $\approx$50%; erythema multiforme or other rash; myalgia and arthralgia; bullous myringitis; and nausea and vomiting — diarrhoea is unusual and transient if it occurs.

Diagnosis is principally serological as the organisms are not visible on a Gram stain and culture is difficult and specialized. The course is often protracted but response to erythromycin or tetracycline is usual.

42. CALCIFIED LESIONS ON THE CHEST X-RAY   ABDE

Asbestos exposure may cause pulmonary fibrosis, calcific pleural plaques, bronchogenic carcinoma and mesothelioma.

Histoplasma capsulatum is a fungus and the main endemic area is central USA, though the organism is also found in South America, Africa, and Asia. Infections may be: i) asymptomatic; ii) primary cutaneous; iii) acute or chronic pulmonary infections – chronic infections may be associated with calcific histoplasmomas; and iv) disseminated systemic infections. Many infections are self-limiting but treatment with amphotericin B may be necessary for chronic pulmonary and disseminated infections.

Apart from calcification of the mitral valve itself, chronic cases of mitral valve disease may be associated with pulmonary haemosiderosis. Other cardiac causes of calcification include calcified aortic knuckle and calcification of the pericardium (tuberculous).

Calcific foci as a late consequence of chicken pox pneumonitis are very rare.

Other conditions in which calcific lesions may be seen on a chest radiograph include:
Pulmonary causes
    Bronchogenic carcinoma
    Silicosis – egg shell calcification
    Sarcoidosis – in hilar nodes and rarely in parenchyma
    Chronic empyema
    TB – Gohn focus
Extrapulmonary causes
    Progressive systemic sclerosis
    Hyperparathyroidism
    Dermatomyositis.
    Cysticercosis

43. FIBROSING ALVEOLITIS ABCE

Fibrosing alveolitis is characterized by a restrictive lung picture. Thus the FEV_1 and FVC are reduced proportionately. Changes in vital capacity (VC), which crudely reflect changes in lung compliance, may be used to monitor disease progression. The VC and the transfer factor (Tl_{CO}) decrease as the disease progresses. Exertional hypoxia is usual whereas hypoxia and hypocapnia (due to compensatory hyperventilation) at rest are late features.

44. SYNDROME OF INAPPROPRIATE SECRETION OF ANTI-DIURETIC HORMONE C

The causes of inappropriate ADH secretion include: malignancy, intracranial pathology, chest disease, psychoses and drugs.

The biochemical picture is essentially dilutional. The diagnosis is based on a urine osmolality greater than that of the plasma with an inappropriate urinary sodium loss, of the order of >20-50 mmol per 24 hours, despite hyponatraemia.

Patients may be asymptomatic or hyponatraemia may be associated with headache, confusion, seizures and coma according to its severity.

Management — treatment of the underlying cause plus water deprivation in the well motivated and symptomatic patient, or dimethylchlortetracycline which antagonises the renal response to ADH.

See February 1990 question 3.

45. CARCINOID SYNDROME ABE

Carcinoid tumours are numerically and clinically most important in the midgut. The carcinoid tumour secretes 5 hydroxytryptamine (5HT) (serotonin) for which tryptophan is the fundamental substrate. Niacin (nicotinic acid) is present in most foods and may also be synthesized from tryptophan. Deficiency of niacin results in pellagra and this may be precipitated in patients with carcinoid syndrome through competition for tryptophan. Isoniazid treatment and Hartnup disease may also be associated with niacin deficency.

The main clinical feature of carcinoid syndrome is flushing, which may persist for many hours or days and may be provoked by alcohol, stress or meals. Wheezing, vasodilatation with a tachycardia and hypotension, urticarial rashes and diarrhoea are also common. Valvular fibrosis typically involves the tricuspid and pulmonary valves but may occur on left sided valves in the presence of a right-left shunt (or where there is a primary bronchial carcinoid).

The cardinal features of pellagra are diarrhoea, dermatitis, dementia and death.

Peptic ulceration is said to be commoner in patients with carcinoid syndrome.

The principal metabolite of hydroxytryptamine is 5 hydroxy indole acetic acid which is utilised in a diagnostic assay on the urine.

The carcinoid syndrome with a primary in the terminal ileum necessitates hepatic metastases as 5HT released from the primary tumour will be extensively metabolized during the hepatic first pass and removal of the primary alone, which typically constitutes $\approx 1\%$ of the tumour bulk, is of no relevance. Occasionally, if these metastases are few or located in one lobe of the liver, surgical excision is beneficial. Embolization of large masses of hepatic metastases risks precipitating a carcinoid crisis.

Useful, non-surgical, treatments include:
   5HT antagonists — methysergide and cyproheptadine
   Alpha receptor blockade — phenoxybenzamine and phenothiazines
   Somatostatin used pre-operatively and for 'carcinoid crises'
   Histamine 1 and 2 receptor blockade — gastric tumours secrete histamine
   Codeine phosphate for diarrhoea

Note: As dementia is a feature of pellagra and carcinoid syndrome is known to precipitate pellagra it could be argued that dementia is a recognized feature of the carcinoid syndrome.

46. HEPATITIS B CARRIER   ABE

The hepatitis B carrier state complicates ≈5-10% of all infections. It may be asymptomatic or cause chronic persistent hepatitis, chronic active hepatitis, or cirrhosis. There is a marked concordance between hepatocellular carcinoma and the hepatitis B carrier state, independent of whether there is cirrhosis or not. Hepatitis B is associated with both membranous and, less commonly, membranoproliferative (mesangiocapillary) nephropathy. The delta agent is a defective hepatitis virus which requires the hepatitis B virus for survival. It is relatively rare in the West, apart from in intravenous drug abusers, but is common in parts of Africa, the Far East, South America and Russia. Co-infection, i.e. simultaneous infection with the two viruses, generally poses no extra risk for the patient as the hepatitis B virus is expelled in the majority of cases and the delta agent can no longer survive. Super-infection with the delta virus, i.e. on top of an established hepatitis B infection, is much more serious and predisposes to progressive hepatic damage in 70-90% of cases.

Note: on nomenclature: 'Non-A Non-B hepatitis' has recently been sub-divided into hepatitis C (classical, parenteral variety) and hepatitis E (epidemic, enteral variety). Hepatitis F has also been described.

47. PRIMARY BILIARY CIRROSIS   AD

Primary biliary cirrhosis mainly affects women in late middle age. Apart from mild jaundice and hepatosplenomegaly, pruritus is a prominent early feature and may be precipitated or exacerbated by pregnancy or the oral contraceptive pill. Bone pain in the back and ribs, due to nutritional osteomalacia, cutaneous xanthomata, particularly peri-orbital xanthelasma and clubbing are common later in the course of the disease. There may be clinical manifestations of associated diseases e.g. rheumatoid arthritis, dermatomyositis and CREST syndrome, and renal involvement includes renal tubular acidosis and membranous nephropathy. Hepatic histology mainly reflects bile duct damage in the early stages with an inflammatory peri-ductal infiltrate, often with granulomata, and later fibrosis, ductular proliferation, scarring and cirrhosis. The clinical and histological diagnosis may be supported by the presence of anti-mitochondrial antibodies in >90% of cases. An increased concentration of circulating IgM is also common. Management is largely that of chronic liver disease. Pruritus may be relieved by cholestyramine but is seldom tolerated in adequate doses by the patients. Vitamin D supplements may be necessary. Recently ursodeoxycholic acid (Ursodiol), traditionally used to dissolve gall stones, and cyclosporin A have been shown to improve liver biochemistry in pre-cirrhotic patients. Longer term follow-up is needed to ascertain whether there is also any improvement, or delayed progression, of liver histology. Contrary to early reports, steroids and penicillamine are not effective and steroids in particular should be avoided as they are likely to exacerbate bone disease.

Anti neutrophil cytoplasmic antibodies (ANCA) are associated with systemic (small vessel) vasculitis. They are typically identified in patient's serum by an indirect immunofluorescent technique using fixed neutrophils and FITC-labelled anti-human light chains (kappa and lambda) as substrate and secondary antibody layer respectively. Two major patterns of immunofluorescence are recognized, perinuclear (p) and cytoplasmic (c). The precise ligands giving these patterns, for the vast majority of antibodies, are now known and form the basis of more specific assay techniques. Antibodies with p-ANCA specificity are directed against myeloperoxidase and segregate mainly with micropolyarteritis but also polyarteritis nodosa and Churg-Strauss syndrome. Antibodies with c-ANCA specificity are directed against a cytoplasmic enzyme designated proteinase-3 (which is likely to be myeloblastin), and segregate mainly with Wegener's granulomatosis, although patients with clinical micropolyarteritis are also often c-ANCA positive.

48. AMOEBIC LIVER ABSCESS   ABC

Entamoeba histolytica is typically a wholly intraluminal commensal organism.

Hepatic abscesses may occur in patients with no evidence of amoebic dysentery and presentation is typically of fever, weight loss and right hypochondrial pain. Examination will confirm tender hepatomegaly. There may be a sympathetic right basal pleural effusion or consolidation. Liver biochemistry is typically only mildly deranged with modest increases in both amino transpeptidases and liver alkaline phosphatase. A neutrophil leucocytosis, increased erythrocyte sedimentation rate and a normochromic normocytic anaemia are usual. In the majority of cases the cyst is single and may be demonstrated on ultrasound or on a CT scan. The liver abscess may form fistulae into the right lung, peritoneum, pericardium or cutaneously.

The diagnosis of amoebic infection is confirmed by the demonstration of trophozoites containing ingested red blood cells in stool, biopsy specimens, and aspirate from hepatic cysts. Serological tests are mainly useful in a negative sense as a positive result does not differentiate acute from previous infection.

Metronidazole is the treatment of choice for amoebiasis whatever its manifestation. Drainage of a hepatic abscess is only appropriate where a superficial abscess is large and threatens rupture into adjacent tissues. It is contraindicated where there are multiple cysts.

49. CONN'S SYNDROME   AB

Conn's syndrome (primary hyperaldosteronism) is usually due to a solitary adrenal adenoma: rarely, this is malignant. The syndrome may also be caused by bilateral hyperplasia of the zona glomerulosa. The main site of action of aldosterone is the distal tubule and collecting duct where Na^+ retention at the expense of K^+ and H^+ loss gives the characteristic biochemical picture of mild hypernatraemia, hypokalaemia and a metabolic alkalosis. Na^+ retention is responsible for H_2O retention and therefore hypertension. Patients are not clinically fluid overloaded by virtue of the, unexplained, 'escape phenomenon' in which critical extra-cellular fluid expansion causes reduced Na^+ reabsorption in the proximal (sic) tubule and thus an effective natriuresis despite the persistent mineralocorticoid effect. Hypokalaemia manifests as both muscle weakness and polyuria (and hence polydypsia). The accompanying alkalosis may reduce the ionized Ca^{2+} and predispose to paraesthesiae and tetany. Mild hyperglycaemia may occur. In Conn's syndrome, renin secretion is suppressed by salt and water retention.

The diagnosis of Conn's syndrome is based on the biochemical picture with demonstration of increased aldosterone which is not suppressed by a high salt intake and a low plasma renin which is not increased by a low salt intake or adoption of an erect posture.

It may be possible to visualize a single adenoma by ultrasound scan, angiography or a CT scan, but bilateral adrenal vein catheterization and measurement of aldosterone levels is the best technique for differentiating adrenal hyperplasia from an adenoma.

Both adenomas and hyperplasia may be managed with spironolactone (an aldosterone antagonist). Surgical removal of adenomas is usually curative.

50. **PRIMARY HYPOTHYROIDISM**   **ABCE**

Primary myxoedema is approximately ten times less common than hyperthyroidism. It is usually a consequence of autoimmune thyroiditis (Hashimoto's disease) though other causes include:
  I_2 deficiency
  Congenital e.g. agenesis or enzyme deficiencies such as Pendred's syndrome
  Goitrogens e.g. Li^{3+}, F^-, I_2, sulphonamides, phenyl butazone, brassicas
  Iatrogenic — surgery, I^{131}, anti-thyroid drugs
  Tumour

Clinical features include:
  i)   Lethargy — both mental and physical
  ii) Weight gain with loss of appetite
  iii) Mucopolysaccharide infiltration of the skin and vocal cords give the characteristic coarse facies and gruff voice
  iv) alopecia with dry, brittle hair
  v)   menorrhagia
  vi) arthralgia
  vii) serositis with pericardial and pleural effusions (transudates) and ascites
  viii) cardiac — bradycardia, angina and CCF
  ix) neurology — carpal tunnel syndrome, peripheral neuropathy, myopathy and myotonia, cerebellar syndrome, myxoedema madness, and coma
  x)   hypercarotenaemia

xi) hypercholesterolaemia
xii) hyperprolactinaemia
xiii) biochemically — increased transaminases, creatinine kinase
and CSF protein.

Histologically, in Hashimoto's thyroiditis, the gland shows a mixture of cellular infiltrate, lymphoid follicles and fibrosis and with time the latter predominates.

The diagnosis is made on the basis of a reduced (free) T4 concentration and an increased concentration of TSH. Anti-microsomal and thyroglobulin antibodies are characteristic in Hashimoto's thyroiditis but are also found in other thyroid disorders and may occur in the absence of any thyroid abnormality. Other autoimmune disorders are common, for example, approximately 25% will have parietal cell antibodies and 10% will develop pernicious anaemia.

51. ACROMEGALY   ABDE

Acromegaly is due to excessive secretion of growth hormone (GH) (somatotrophic hormone) from a pituitary eosinophilic (acidophilic) adenoma. In a minority of cases this is a microscopic adenoma. More usually, there is expansion of the pituitary fossa and disease manifestations are due to local mechanical effects and systemic effects.

Local effects
i)   compression of optic nerve(s)/chiasma — the characteristic field defect, although virtually every combination is possible, is a bilateral temporal upper quadrantic hemianopia as fibres from the inferior medial retina are usually the first to be compressed
ii) suprasellar extension may lead to diabetes insipidus and hypopituitarism. (LH and FSH are lost before ACTH + TSH)
iii) headaches

Systemic effects
i)   bone overgrowth giving the characteristic expansion of the skull and jaw with wide separation of the teeth, plus vertebral enlargement with kyphosis
ii) soft tissue expansion and visceromegaly with fleshy features, spade like hands and feet, and enlargement of the tongue,

heart, liver and thyroid gland

iii) hormonal — anti-insulin effect with a reduction in the number of insulin receptors causing glucose intolerance, galactorrhoea due to hyperprolactinaemia

iv) hypertension;

v) osteoporosis

vi) chondrocalcinosis

vii) neurological — carpal tunnel syndrome and other entrapment neuropathies

viii) myopathy

ix) association with MEN type I.

Investigations may show:

Pituitary function tests

Increased GH (the concentration of which is a poor marker of disease activity), and increased prolactin concentration in 25% of cases.

Failure of growth hormone levels to supress with an oral glucose tolerance test

An increase in GH secretion in response to a TRH test (normals do not respond).

Bromocriptine and L-dopa cause an increase in GH in acromegalics and a reduction in normals

Evidence of hypopituitarism

Radiology

Plain radiographs may show expansion of the pituitary fossa with a double floor and erosion of the posterior clinoids

High resolution CT scans will show most microadenomas and may be combined with metrizamide cisternography to demonstrate any suprasellar extension of the tumour

Biochemistry

Increase in GFR

Hypercalcaemia and hypercalciuria

Hyperphosphataemia

Increased alkaline phosphatase (associated with increased PTH).

Treatment options include:

surgical — trans-sphenoidal hypophysectomy or removal of a microadenoma

radiotherapy — yttrium-90 implantation or external radiotherapy

medical — bromocriptine.

52. PRURITUS   ABCDE

Causes of pruritus include:
obstructive jaundice
chronic renal failure
iron deficiency anaemia
myeloproliferative disorders
lymphoma
carcinoma
hypo/hyper thyroidism
allergies
parasites e.g. threadworm
tabes dorsalis
dermatological disorders e.g. scabies, dermatitis herpetiformis,
contact dermatitis, lichen simplex

53. POST-STREPTOCOCCAL GLOMERULONEPHRITITIS   ABDE

Post-streptococcal glomerulonephritis is primarily a disease of
children in non-developed countries. It may follow either post-
streptococcal throat or skin infections. A latent period of between 7
and 40 days separates the onset of clinical nephritis from the acute
infection, though microscopic haematuria and proteinuria may occur
during this period. Approximately 15% of patients will develop
glomerulonephritis. The vast majority of these are subclinical and are
diagnosed on the basis of a proven preceding streptococcal infection
with haematuria, and a reduction in the serum complement.
Approximately 10% of patients have the typical tetrad of an acute
nephritic syndrome: haematuria, oedema (including pulmonary),
oliguria and hypertension. Rarely (0.5%) hypertensive
encephalopathy may precipitate coma and convulsions. Moderate
proteinuria is usual but a nephrotic syndrome is rare. Lumbar
discomfort and nausea and vomiting are common.

Rarely, rapidly progressive glomerulonephritis (RPGN) may
intervene.
Investigations may show:
Bacteriology – anti-streptolysin O titres (ASOT) are maximal 3-5
weeks after the acute infection.
Immunology – most patients have a polyclonal increase in IgG and

IgM antibodies, the C3 component of complement is reduced in up to
90% of patients early in the course of the disease, due to activation of
the alternative pathway, and more rarely C4 and C2 concentrations are
reduced indicating activation of complement by the classical pathway,
cryoglobulins may also be demonstrated.

Pathology — typically renal histology shows a mesangioproliferative
glomerulonephritis (rarely a diffuse crescentic picture). Electron
microscopy may show characteristic sub-epithelial 'humps' (though
sub-endothelial and intramembranous deposits also occur),
immunofluorescence is likely to show discontinuous granular
deposition of C3, IgM and IgG.

Treatment — effective antibiotic treatment of proven streptococcal
infection with prophylactic antibiotics for sibling contacts will prevent
post-streptococcal glomerulonephritis. Treatment of established
nephritis is conventional management of fluid and electrolytes (salt and
water restriction, dialysis if necessary), and treatment of hypertension.
Most series, but not all, suggest that there are no long term sequelae
to this illness.

The co-existence of renal disease and hypocomplementaemia is seen
in:
  Lupus nephritis
  Sub-acute bacterial endocarditis
  Shunt nephritis
  Mesangiocapillary (membranoproliferative) glomerulonephritis
  types I and II (associated with C3-nephritic factor)
  Mixed essential cryoglobulinaemia (C4 and C2)
  Cholesterol emboli.

54. AMYLOIDOSIS   C

The two principal types of renal amyloid deposits are
  i) AA — ('Secondary' or Non-Immunocyte Related) this is
      associated with inflammatory processes such as chronic sepsis
      or rheumatoid arthritis in which serum amyloid-A (SAA) is
      the serum precursor of the AA deposits. Classically, the
      organs involved are the liver, kidney, spleen, heart, gut and
      adrenal glands
  ii) AL — ('Primary' or Immunocyte Related) this is associated

with light chain deposition e.g. from multiple myeloma and non-malignant gammopathies (cryoglobulinaemia does *not* predispose to amyloidosis). The heart, tongue, gastrointestinal tract, nerves and skin are typically involved, with renal involvement in ≈20% of cases.

Serum amyloid protein P (SAP) is a virtually ubiquitous amyloid protein and this has been utilized in the development of a non-invasive isotope scan to characterize tissue involvement in patients with either type of amyloidosis.

Clinical features of amyloidosis are those of the organ system involved: macroglossia; thyroglossia; cutaneous infiltrates; cardiomegaly and CCF; hepatomegaly — typically with no abnormalities of hepatic biochemistry; peripheral and autonomic neuropathy; renal disease is characterized by enlargement of the kidneys, nephrotic range proteinuria, renal impairment in >50% of patients at the time of presentation, tubular dysfunction e.g. renal tubular acidosis and Fanconi syndrome, and a urinary sediment with abundant casts, but very rarely red cells or red cell casts (fat bodies are a common finding in any renal disease associated with heavy proteinuria). Urinary histology demonstrates mesangial deposits of amyloid (which *must* be confirmed e.g. by apple-green bi-refringence when stained with congo-red and viewed under polarized light, or using immuno fluorescent-peroxidase techniques), especially in AA amyloid, with little cellular infiltrate. M. myeloma associated disease shows laminated 'ground glass' tubular casts. Thickening of the arterial media is a prominent early finding.

Treatment of amyloidosis is primarily that of the underlying disease plus conventional treatment of its manifestations. AL amyloid has a significantly worse prognosis compared with AA amyloid.

55. ACID-BASE ABNORMALITIES C

Type I (distal) renal tubular acidosis is the classical condition in which there is an inability to acidify the urine normally.

Lithium therapy causes nephrogenic diabetes insipidus by desensitizing the distal convoluted tubule and collecting duct to the effects of vasopressin (ADH). Patients are able to excrete a water load normally but are unable to concentrate their urine in conditions of fluid depletion. Thiazide diuretics reduce the resulting polyuria and polydypsia by relative salt and water depletion and thus increasing the fractional absorption of salt and water in the proximal tubule – this treatment should be used with caution however as lithium excretion is reduced and toxicity may ensue. Distal tubular disease may also contribute to a defect of urinary acidification in a minority of patients and in a few this may be severe enough to prevent acidification of the urine to < 5.2 following ingestion of an acid load. In the majority of cases, the renal effects of lithium therapy resolve rapidly on stopping the drug. There remains controversy as to whether chronic lithium ingestion causes chronic renal damage: a recent long term (up to 20 years) study suggests that, in the absence of any episodes of lithium toxicity, there are no long term sequelae.

In cranial diabetes insipidus there is no direct effect on renal tubular acid/base homeostasis.

In chronic respiratory failure, there will be compensatory metabolic alkalosis achieved by increased ammoniagenesis.

In chronic renal failure, acid-base changes only occur when the GFR has fallen to < 50% of normal, and compensation typically remains satisfactory to a GFR of ≈10ml/min. The nature of the acid base disturbance will vary to some extent according to the renal disease. A mild degree of HCO_3^- wasting is common but under steady state levels – i.e. in the absence of HCO_3^- loading – urinary acidification is normal (as per proximal renal tubular acidosis) and throughout the progression of chronic renal failure, the urinary pH is < 5.5. In the early stages of chronic renal failure there is considerable adaption by the remaining functioning nephrons which increase their NH_4^- excretion by up to four-fold. With moderate CRF (creatinine 150-300μ mol/l), there is a reduction in [HCO_3] to low-normal concentrations and a compensatory increase in Cl^- such that there is a normal anion gap acidosis. As chronic renal failure progresses (creatinine >300 μmol/l), [HCO_3] falls, typically to a stable level of 12-15 mmol/l, and an increased anion gap acidosis intervenes due to the accumulation of non-excreted organic and inorganic (sulphuric and phosphoric) acid. This is buffered almost wholly by $CaCO_3$ in bone with a minor contribution from respiratory alkalosis.

56. GONORRHOEA   ABCE

Gonnorrhoea in males is characterized by dysuria and a purulent urethral discharge, though a minority of cases are asymptomatic. Rarely the course of the disease may be complicated by epididymitis or stricture formation.

Homosexual males are also prone to proctitis and oropharyngeal infection.

Gonorrhoea in females typically affects the endocervix, urethra and rectum and is asymptomatic in the majority of cases. Trichomoniasis is a very common accompaniment. The infection may be complicated locally by Bartholinitis and vulvitis, and rarely by pelvic inflammatory disease (PID) in which both Fallopian tubes are typically involved.

Systemic gonococcal infection may cause:
   i) joint involvement ranging from a mild arthralgia with little constitutional upset, to a severe asymmetrical destructive oligo-arthritis with a predilection for knee, ankle, shoulder, sternoclavicular and temperomandibular joints
   ii) tenosynovitis is usual
   iii) a painful papular petechial pustular rash
   iv) perihepatitis (Curtis Fitz-Hugh syndrome) — usually in women with PID
   v) meningitis
   vi) endocarditis.

Diagnosis is by demonstration of Gram negative diplococci +/- culture. Treatment is traditionally penicillin but resistant organisms are common and alternatives include: Septrin, erythromycin, cefuroxime and tetracyclines.

57. NORMAL MILESTONES   CE

The grasp reflex disappears at 2-3 weeks. The baby will hold objects at 12 weeks, will grasp them from 20 weeks (progressing from a radial to an ulnar grip) and will be picking up small objects by opposition of the thumb and forefinger by 9 months.

The walking reflex appears at 6-8 weeks and by 24 weeks the baby will be able to support its own weight. By 36 weeks it will pull itself to its feet, and by 48 weeks, after a period of 'cruising around the furniture' will be able to walk.

Voluntary bladder control only starts to develop after 15 months and by 18 months most children will be 'dry' during the day.

Cup and spoon feeding starts after 15 months.

Although the baby will be able to say "no" with meaning at about 10 months, it will not be linking words until late in its second year.

58. SCROTAL SWELLINGS   ABCDE

Orchioblastoma (not orchidoblastoma) is now known as a yolk sac carcinoma (endodermal sinus tumour). It is far and away the most common childhood testicular tumour and usually develops between infancy and the age of 5. The prognosis is very good.

59. RIGHT-SIDED ABDOMINAL PAIN IN A 4 YEAR OLD   ABCE

Shigella. sonnei is the main pathogen of the *Shigella* genus in Britain, though *Sh. dysenteriae* and *Sh. flexneri* are more common world-wide. The organisms are robust and spread rapidly in conditions of dirt and overcrowding. *Shigella* spp. cause a locally invasive colitis, most severe in *Sh. dysenteriae*. Clinical disease, following 2-7 days incubation, ranges from trivial short-lived diarrhoea to a more severe illness with diarrhoea containing blood stained mucus ('red-currant jelly') and pus, lower abdominal pain (as may *Campylobacter* and *Salmonella*), fever and either leucocytosis or leucopenia. Rarely, shigellosis may manifest as a seronegative spondarthritis. Children may also exhibit a severe meningitis and are prone to appendicitis and intussusception.

Diagnosis — culture.

Treatment — often none is necessary. In more severe cases, fluid and electrolyte replacement and ampicillin, Septrin or tetracycline.

Ascariasis is typically asymptomatic whilst the adult worms reside in the ileum. It may, however, delay development in infected children, and migration of the larval stages through the lungs may cause Loeffler's syndrome i.e. pneumonitis and eosinophilia. More severe disease may be caused by large numbers of worms occluding the bowel, appendix, or biliary tree.

Diagnosis is made by demonstrating eggs in the faeces or identifying intact worms.

Treatment is with piperazine, mebendazole, pyrantel or levamisole

Acute pyelonephritis may present with fever, vomiting and right-sided abdominal pain. Lobar pneumonia may also present with fever, systemic upset and abdominal pain.

60. NORMAL PUBERTY   ABDE

In boys, the testis and scrotum enlarge first, and the scrotum becomes darker, followed by lengthening and the widening of the penis. Pubic and then axillary hair develop later. Increase in size of the areola is normal and less commonly tender gynaecomastia develops. This usually regresses after a year or so.

In girls, development of the breast bud is followed by enlargement of the areola and projection of the papilla beyond the normal breast contour, and finally the smooth contoured adult breast. Pubic hair grows first on the labia and then the mons and may precede or follow breast development.

Acne vulgaris and a diffuse thyroid enlargement are common consequences of puberty.

1. UVEITIS   **BCDE**

Clinically, iritis is characterized by pain, blurred vision, 'muddy' iris, hypopyon and corneal injection.

Treatment — specific treatment of the underlying disease, topical steroids mydriatics and an eyepatch.

See February 1990 question 13.

2. CHRONIC LEG ULCERATION   **ABCD**

Causes of leg ulceration include
   Gravitational (venous) ulcers
   Trauma
   Arterial — hypertension, atheroma
   Vasculitis — Wegener's granulomatosis, cryoglobulinaemia,
                rheumatoid arthritis
   Pyoderma gangrenosum
   Neoplasia
   Necrobiosis lipoidica
   Haematological — thrombocythaemia, polycythaemia, hereditary
                spherocytois, sickle cell disease
   Neuropathic — diabetes, leprosy, syringomyelia, and tertiary syphilis.

3. HUNTINGTON'S DISEASE   **ABE**

Huntington's disease shows full penetrance. The tight linkage to genetic markers in 4p16.3 has facilitated screening for the disease though this facility has been a focus of much controversy. New mutations are almost unknown. The brain lesion localizes primarily to the caudate nucleus and putamen which show considerable atrophy with loss of GABA-ergic and cholinergic neurones. There is usually a lesser degree of cortical atrophy. Clinical disease typically starts in middle age (30-50) with a change in personality, not dissimilar to a frontal lobe syndrome, followed by dementia or a psychotic state. Chorea is usual but may be replaced by an akinetic-rigid state later in the course of the disease. Children with Huntington's chorea, usually inherited from the father, may present with the so-called Westphal variant in which an akinetic-rigid syndrome and dementia are prominent, and epilepsy is common.

4.   HUMAN LEUCOCYTE ANTIGENS (HLA)   ACE

The major histocompatability complex (MHC) proteins in man are referred to as human leucocyte (not lymphocyte) antigens, reflecting the cell type to which they are most closely associated.

MHC class I molecules (A, B and C) are heterodimers of a heavy chain (comprising alpha 1, 2 and 3 domains) plus $\beta2$ microglobulin, and are primarily responsible for presentation of viral antigens to cytotoxic T lymphocytes. They are virtually ubiquitous on nucleated cells — and indeed are found in low numbers on red cells, although the RCP are broadly correct in stating that they are not.

MHC class II molecules (DR, DP and DQ) are heterodimers of an α and a β chain and are primarily responsible for presentation of antigen by antigen presenting cells to T helper cells, though at present only the DR molecule has a well defined role. MHC class II molecules are limited to selected cell populations e.g. activated T lymphocytes, B lymphocytes, macrophages and activated endothelial cells. The third group of MHC genes, class III, encode certain complement components. All three gene segments are localized to the short arm of chromosome 6 and, as you would expect, everyone bears two alleles of each gene. The HLA genes inherited from each parent are referred to as a haplotype. MHC molecules show very marked polymorphism and inter-ethnic variability of HLA genes has proved to be a valuable tool in plotting population migrations. An unfortunate corollary of possession of these highly promiscuous HLA determinants, is their ability to stimulate an immune response in an HLA mismatched host. There is extensive and convincing literature demonstrating that donor/recipient HLA matching improves the outcome of solid organ transplants and in the case of bone marrow transplants, a complete HLA match is essential to minimize the risk of graft versus host disease.

5. RADIAL NERVE   BCE

The muscles supplied by the radial nerve are: triceps, anconeus, brachioradialis, and extensor carpi radialis longus and brevis. The deep branch of the radial nerve innervates supinator, extensor digitorum, extensor digiti minimi, extensor carpi ulnaris and extensor carpi radialis brevis, and its posterior interosseus branch supplies abductor pollicis longus, extensor pollicis longus and brevis, and extensor indicis.

Sensory supply is via the posterior brachial cutaneous nerve to the back of the arm, via the lower lateral brachial cutaneous nerve to the lower lateral arm and via the posterior antebrachial cutaneous nerve to the dorsal forearm.

The most frequent injury is sustained as the so-called 'Saturday night paralysis' in which the nerve is compressed, as it winds around the middle third of the humerus, against a chair back. The triceps is spared but all distal muscles are paralysed and there is sensory loss over the dorsum of the hand. Recovery typically occurs over a period of a few weeks.

6. ACTION POTENTIAL   ACD

The resting state of nerve (and muscle) cells is characterized by Na^+ being actively transported out and K^+ actively transported into the cell. During depolarization, the cell membrane becomes momentarily very permeable to the inward flow of Na^+ until the firing point is achieved at which point the cell discharges its action potential. The minimum stimulus to achieve discharge gives an identical action potential to any greater stimulus — hence the 'all or nothing response'. Velocity of conduction is increased in large diameter fibres and in myelinated nerve fibres.

7. HYPOCALCAEMIA   BCDE

The total serum calcium is the product of both bound and ionised calcium concentrations. It is corrected, somewhat arbitrarily, for an albumin of 40 g/l allowing 0.02 mmol/l for every g/l of albumin either side of this figure. Ionized calcium is available for metabolic processes and is thus the more useful measurement. Hyperventilation will reduce the *ionized* calcium concentration, without altering the total calcium concentration, as an increase in pH ionizes more albumin and Ca^{2+} binds to the extra protein anion.

The only common causes of hypocalcaemia are hypoparathyroidism, osteomalacia/rickets and chronic renal failure.
Rare causes include:
hypomagnesaemia — by inhibition of both PTH secretion and its effect on bone
pseudohypoparathyroidism — in which there is end-organ resistance to the effects of PTH (associated with short stature and neck, moon face, and short 4th and 5th metacarpals)
acute pancreatitis — and this may be due to Ca^{2+} binding to lipids digested by pancreatic enzymes, hypoalbuminaemia or effects on PTH
cis-platinum therapy by causing tubular damage and thus hypomagnesaemia.

8.   ELEVATED PLASMA AMYLASE   ABCDE

Causes of acute pancreatitis include
   Gallstones
   Alcohol
   Abdominal surgery / ERCP / trauma
   Viral infections e.g. mumps
   Hyperparathyroidism and other causes of hypercalcaemia
   Hyperlipidaemia
   Drugs — diuretics, azathioprine, phenformin, pill and high dose steroids
   Hypothermia

Amylase is renally excreted and accumulates in renal failure.
The complications of pancreatitis include abnormalities of glucose intolerance ranging from the trivial to diabetic ketoacidosis.

9. **CHOLESTEROL**   **ABCD**

Total plasma cholesterol correlates well with low density lipoprotein (LDL) cholesterol up to the age of about 60. LDL concentrations in excess of 6.6-7 mmol/l significantly predispose to coronary artery disease (also confirmed by reducing the frequency of cardiac events in effectively treated patients).

Antihypertensive drugs may have a deleterious, neutral or beneficial effect on serum lipids. Thiazides and loop diuretics increase total cholesterol, LDL cholesterol and triglycerides. β-blockers (without β_2 agonist properties) increase triglycerides and reduce high density lipoproteins (HDL), (HDL have a protective effect). Calcium antagonists, ACE inhibitors and labetolol have no effect. Alpha-blockers have a beneficial effect by both reducing LDL and increasing HDL.

Interruption of the enterohepatic circulation of bile salts is the basis of treatment of hyper-cholesterolaemia with cholestyramine. This binds to bile acids in the gastrointestinal tract and thus promotes their regeneration from cholesterol. This is paralleled by an increase in hepatic LDL receptors and the catabolism of LDL.

10. **TRICYCLIC ANTIDEPRESSANTS**   **ABCDE**

Mild toxicity manifests as drowsiness, xerostomia, mydriasis, strabismus and hyperreflexia. More severe poisoning may cause: cardiorespiratory suppression with hypoxia and metabolic and respiratory acidosis; hypothermia; quinidine-like effects cause prolongation of the QRS complex and tachyarrhythmias; coma; convulsions; ileus; and urinary retention.

Treatment is gastric lavage and activated charcoal.

Arrhythmias seldom require specific treatment and indeed anti-arrhythmic drugs may potentiate the toxic effects. Seizures should be treated with intravenous diazepam or heminevrin (with airway supervision).

See June 1990 question 22.

11. DELAYED HYPERSENSITIVITY   BCDE

Type I (anaphylactic) hypersensitivity occurs when pre-formed antibodies (IgE) bound to mast cells encounter their specific ligand and stimulate the mast cells to degranulate releasing histamine, leukotrienes, serotonin, and kinins e.g. atopic processes.

Type II (cytotoxic) hypersensitivity occurs when antigen bound to the target tissue engages IgG or IgM antibody with subsequent tissue destruction e.g. Goodpasture's disease and myasthenia gravis in which auto-antibodies are directed against glomerular/alveolar basement membrane and acetylcholine receptor respectively, and auto-immune haemolytic anaemia.

Type III (Arthus reaction) hypersensitivity occurs when antigen-antibody complexes in the circulation deposit in tissues with subsequent complement activation and inflammatory cell invasion e.g. serum sickness, rheumatoid arthritis, some forms of glomerulo-nephritis.

Type IV (cell mediated) hypersensitivity is due to the action of antigen specific T cells e.g. tuberculosis, basis of Heaf and Kveim tests, contact dermatitis.

Type V hypersensitivity in which antibodies are stimulatory e.g. Grave's disease.

Type VI hypersensitivity in which K-cells (Killer cells) lyse targets coated with antibody e.g. tumours and helminths.

Antihuman, usually horse or rabbit, lymphocyte globulin rapidly clears the blood of virtually all circulating lymphocytes.

Di George syndrome, Nezelof's syndrome, Swiss type combined immunodeficiency and Wisckott Aldrich syndrome are congenital conditions in which cell mediated responses are affected. AIDS is probably the commonest cause of impaired T cell function.

12. PULMONARY PARASITIC INFECTION   ABDE

Ascaris lumbricoides — ingested eggs hatch in the ileum, larvae penetrate the mucosa and achieve the pulmonary circulation, via the portal circulation, where they may precipitate a pneumonitis. Larvae ascend the bronchi and trachea and thus re-enter the gastrointestinal tract (GIT) to become mature worms.

Ancylostoma duodenale and *Necator americanus* are the main forms of hookworm. *A. duodenale* usually enters the host via the skin or more rarely is ingested. Interstitial pneumonitis is unusual and only occurs in the event of a heavy primary infestation.

Echinococcus granulosus eggs are ingested, hatch in the duodenum and larvae penetrate the mucosa and pass in the portal circulation and lymphatic vessels to the liver and lungs to form hydatid cysts.

Schistosoma haematobium, mansoni and *japonicum* have different clinical features but similar life cycles. Cercariae attach to and penetrate the skin, migrate to the lungs and pass from there to the liver. Mature worms then migrate along vessels to venules along the gastrointestinal tract in the case of *S. mansoni* and *japonicum,* and the bladder in the case of *S. haematobium.* Eggs passed in urine or faeces hatch as miracidia which penetrate certain species of snail, mature as sporocysts and subsequently shed cercariae.

Taenia solium is usually ingested as the cysticercus stage in pork. This develops into an adult worm in the gastrointestinal tract. Cysticercosis is more unusual in man and is a consequence of ingesting the eggs; invasion of the CNS is characteristic.

13. TOXOPLASMOSIS   ABC

The cat is the definitive host of *Toxoplasma gondii*. Man is infected by ingesting oocytes (excreted by the cat) or by eating inadequately cooked meat containing cysts. In the gut sporozoites are released and multiply in the tissues forming cysts.

Congenital toxoplasmosis in the first trimester may result in abortion. The characteristic features of a surviving infant are microcephaly, chorioretinitis, convulsions and intracerebral calcification, though deafness and mental retardation may intervene later. Posterior uveitis/choroidoretinitis is a late complication of congenital toxoplasmosis (*not* acquired).

Acquired toxoplasmosis varies from an asymptomatic infection in most cases, through a mild viral-type illness, to manifestations including hepatosplenomegaly, lymphadenopathy, myocarditis and encephalitis.

The diagnosis is typically serological (including the Sabin-Feldman dye test) but may be made by demonstration of the parasite in infected tissue.

Treatment, rarely indicated, is with pyrimethamine and sulphonamides.

14. **INFECTIOUS MONONUCLEOSIS**   **BCD**

Infection with Epstein-Barr virus typically affects young adults. Transmission is probably mainly as an aerosol — contrary to popular belief, osculation is not of major importance. The incubation period is of the order of two weeks. The majority of infections are asymptomatic and the spectrum of clinical disease ranges from fever, infected fauces and cervical lymphadenopathy to a more severe presentation with oedema, and palatal petechiae and vesicles. Splenomegaly is common ($\approx 50\%$), whereas clinical jaundice ($< 10\%$) and a rash ($\approx 5\%$) are unusual. Renal involvement manifests as mild, transient uraemia and microscopic haematuria. Pneumonitis, meningitis, mononeuritis multiplex and encephalitis are rare. The mild, transient, non-pruritic rash due to EBV itself cannot be confused with the florid, pruritic, maculopapular rash which is precipitated in most patients by ampicillin. A mild thrombocytopenia is common. Abnormal liver biochemistry is virtually the rule and typically shows a mild hepatitic picture.

The diagnosis may be confirmed serologically (e.g. the Paul-Bunnell test in which heterotrophile antibodies cause agglutination of sheep red cells). Atypical mononuclear cells (derived from T cells) are characteristic but are not diagnostic and are also present in toxoplasmosis, cytomegalovirus, chicken pox, hepatitis A and influenza.

EBV has well characterized associations with malignancy including: Burkitt's lymphoma; nasopharyngeal carcinomas; and lymphoma in immunosuppressed transplant recipients, particularly those receiving cyclosporin A.

Note: a vesicular eruption is a recognized feature of infectious mononucleosis.

15. TYPHOID FEVER   BD

The onset of typhoid is characteristically indolent and non-specific and early symptoms include: headache, abdominal discomfort/pain, generalized aches and pains, fever, epistaxis, and, in children, a cough. Bloody diarrhoea is occasionally an early feature, but typically occurs in the second or third week due to sloughing of Peyer's patches. Other complications include bowel perforation, neuropsychiatric manifestations, pneumonia, nephritis and hepatitis. Examination may reveal: rose-coloured spots — which are flattened papules and *not* petechial — appear in crops and are characteristically sparse (principally found on the abdomen but also the chest and back and sometimes the face); mild hepato-splenomegaly; abdominal distension; furred tongue; and scattered crepitations and ronchi in the chest. A relative bradycardia may be present.

The diagnosis is best made by culture of *salmonella typhi* from stool or blood, the Widal test, i.e. the demonstration of a fourfold increase in antibodies against flagellar (H) or somatic (O) antigens, is less useful. The white cell count is characteristically normal but both mild leucopenia and leucocytosis are described. Abnormal liver biochemistry is common.

The best treatment is amoxycillin. Chloramphenicol, despite the emergence of resistant strains is the mainstay of treatment in non-developed countries. Ampicillin and co-trimoxazole are also effective. A chronic carrier state may occur with persistent infection in the gall bladder, elsewhere in the biliary tree, or occasionally in the renal tract. These should be treated in the first instance with prolonged courses of antibiotics.

16. DISSEMINATED INTRAVASCULAR COAGULATION — BE

This lady has disseminated intravascular coagulation (DIC) complicating eclampsia. She will also be hypertensive, have proteinuria, ankle oedema and will be uraemic and hyperuricaemic.

Investigations will confirm a consumptive coagulopathy (increased PT, KCCT, and FDP's and reduced fibrinogen and platelet count).

The main treatment is immediate delivery of the baby.

In idiopathic thrombocytopenia purpura the prothrombin time is normal.

17. HAEMATOLOGICAL ASSOCIATIONS — BCE

Thrombocytosis is a feature of myeloproliferative, rather than lymphoproliferative, disease. Gout is a recognized complication of haematological disorders associated with increased cell turnover.

Haemolysis (plus recurrent transfusions) in thalassaemia major is the origin of the iron overload.

Down's syndrome is associated with leukaemia.

A number of renal conditions are associated with (true) secondary polycythaemia including: hydronephrosis; renal cell carcinoma; renal artery stenosis; and adult dominant polycystic kidney disease.

18. MACROCYTOSIS — ABD

Apart from conditions predisposing to megaloblastic anaemia (i.e. folate and B_{12} deficiency), which would include jejunal diverticulosis and phenytoin treatment, the causes of macrocytosis include: hypothyroidism; alcohol; liver disease; reticulocytosis from haemolysis or haemorrhage; lympho- and myelo-proliferative disorders; acquired sideroblastic anaemia; respiratory failure; multiple myeloma; and vitamin C deficiency.

19. DRUG ACETYLATION   ABDE

A number of drug reactions are due to inherited enzyme abnormalities, the commonest of which involves N-acetyl-transferase. Two broad phenotypes of the latter are recognized, 'fast' and 'slow' acetylators. Slow acetylators, comprising > 50% of Europeans, may therefore fail to metabolize: hydralazine, isoniazid, dapsone, phenelzine and procainamide. Slow acetylation has been linked to the genesis of hydralazine-induced lupus.

Other enzyme deficiency states adversely affecting drug metabolism include: glucose-6-phosphate dehydrogenase deficiency — this X-linked recessive disorder is characterized by haemolysis following exposure to primaquin, sulphonamides, chloramphenicol, fava beans, nitrofurantoin, quinine, phenacitin, aspirin; and pseudocholinesterase deficiency — necessary for succinylcholine metabolism.

20. THIAZIDE DIURETICS   DE

Thiazide diuretics mainly act on the proximal distal tubule by inhibiting Na^+ reabsorption. Hypokalaemia is due to stimulation of the renin-angiotensin-aldosterone system by the increased delivery of Na^+ to the distal tubule ($Na^+ - K^+$ exchange does occur in the distal tubule, but is not affected directly by thiazides). Thiazide diuretics reduce Ca^{2+} excretion and increase Mg^{2+} clearance, in contrast to loop diuretics, which increase Ca^{2+} excretion and are thus used in the treatment of hypercalcaemia. Thiazides also predispose to glucose intolerance, hyperuricaemia and hypercholesterolaemia.

21. SODIUM VALPROATE   ABC

Recognized side effects of sodium valproate include: hepatic dysfunction, weight gain and thrombocytopenia. Sodium valproate may also cause transient alopecia on initiation of therapy, gastric irritation and pancreatitis.

22. PARKINSON'S SYNDROME

CD

The many causes of a Parkinsonian syndrome include:
i) Parkinson's disease (primary)
ii) Parkinson's-plus syndromes e.g. Steel-Richardson-Olszewski, Shy Drager syndrome
iii) Encephalitis lethargica
iv) Poisons — CO, Mn
v) Drugs — phenothiazines, butyrophenones, reserpine.

Parkinsonian features may be observed in many other global cerebral disorders including: senile and pre-senile dementia; Binswanger's disease (chronic hypertensive encephalopathy); hydrocephalus; and neurosyphilis.

Metaclopramide may occasionally cause an acute extrapyramidal syndrome. This is particularly common in renal failure and therefore it should be used cautiously and in reduced dose in these patients. It responds rapidly to intravenous procyclidine (and other anti-cholinergic drugs).

23. NON STEROIDAL ANTI-INFLAMMATORY DRUGS

ABCD

Most of the renal side effects of anti-inflammatory drugs can be laid squarely at the door of their prostaglandin-inhibiting properties (prostaglandins E2 and F2α are the major renal prostaglandins) and include: vasoconstriction with a corresponding reduction in glomerular filtration; promotion of Na^+, and therefore H_2O, retention (and thus oppose the action of loop diuretics); augmentation of the effect of ADH, and therefore further H_2O retention; and hyporeninaemic-hypoaldosteronism characterized by hyperkalaemia (particularly common in diabetics). Interstitial nephritis is a relatively unusual but well recognized complication and is characterized by nephrotic range proteinuria and in many cases an eosinophilic infiltrate. A reduction in lithium excretion occurs with any cause of renal impairment.

24. CLINICAL TRIALS   CE

The trial may have been very badly designed e.g. were treatment and placebo groups age matched? For example, how were dysmenorrhoea and relief from pain quantitated? It follows that statistical methods are *not* measures of data errors — the statistical result reflects the data analysed whether it is pure fiction or unadulterated fact. The p value, in this instance, establishes that the likelihood of the stated result occurring by chance alone is $< 0.05\%$. It is *not* a measure of the proportion of placebo responses. A p value of 0.05 will include all observations within plus or minus two standard deviations of the mean and this achieves conventional levels of statistical significance.

25. RHEUMATOID ARTHRITIS   ABD

Pleural disease and pleural effusions are not uncommon in rheumatoid disease. The effusion is an exudate with high protein (> 30 g/l) and LDH and low sugar and C3 concentrations. Pulmonary nodules favour the upper lobes and may cavitate and predispose to haemoptysis. Caplan's syndrome is the constellation of multiple large pulmonary nodules and pneumoconiosis. Sub-clinical pulmonary fibrosis is common. A frank fibrosing alveolitis is clinically indistinguishable from primary fibrosing alveolitis and has a similarly poor prognosis. Obstructive airways disease, including the aggressive variant bronchiolitis obliterans, may also occur.

26. SYSTEMIC SCLEROSIS   AE

Organ involvement in progressive systemic sclerosis includes:
  Skin — Raynaud's, sclerodactyly with similar changes elsewhere, telangiectasia, pigmentation and vitiligo, sub-cutaneous calcification especially affecting the finger pulp, and alopecia
  Musculoskeletal — small joint polyarthritis and erosion of terminal phalangeal tufts are common, myopathy and myositis
  Gastrointestinal tract — oesophageal reflux predisposing to strictures, malabsorption and colonic stasis, hepatic dysfunction
  Pulmonary — pulmonary fibrosis, predominantly basal, may progress to cause pulmonary hypertension
  Cardiac — myo- and peri-carditis may occur and conducting

defects are common
Renal — may be very severe and is a late feature (malignant hypertension may develop)

Immunological investigations: include a positive ANF in > 50% with a nucleolar pattern and positive anti-centromere antibodies.

Sacroiliitis is a feature of the seronegative spondarthritides.

A post-cricoid web, which predisposes to malignant change, is a feature of the Plummer-Vinson (Patterson-Kelly-Brown) syndrome associated with chronic iron deficiency anaemia with koilonychia and angular stomatitis

27. PROLONGED QT INTERVAL   ABDE

The normal QT interval is 0.4 seconds.

Causes of a prolonged QT interval include:
   Hypocalcaemia
   Hypomagnasaemia
   Hypokalaemia
   Antiarrhythmic drugs e.g. quinidine, amiodarone
   Lithium
   Hypothermia
   Rheumatic fever
   Ischaemic heart disease
   Diphtheritic heart disease
   Romano Ward syndrome
   Jervell and Lange Nielson syndrome
   Autonomic neuropathy
   Central nervous system disease e.g. subarachnoid haemorrhage, cerebral tumours

The association of hereditary deafness (high tone perceptive) and a prolonged QT interval is seen in the Jervell and Lange Nielson syndrome (Aut R), sudden death due to ventricular arrhythmias is a recognised complication.

28. CEREBRAL ABSCESS   ACD

Paradoxical emboli, from the venous to the arterial system, may occur in transposition of the great vessels, tetralogy of Fallot's and tricuspid atresia. In Fallot's tetralogy it is achieved by the overriding aorta. Tricuspid atresia has many guises but a right left shunt may exist either via an atrial septal defect or by overriding of the aorta. A more conventional right to left shunt through an ASD or VSD in Eisenmenger's syndrome may also, rarely, cause paradoxical emboli (A patent ductus arteriosus usually joins the aorta distal to the left subclavian vein).

29. HYPERTROPHIC CARDIOMYOPATHY   AC

Hypertrophic obstructive cardiomyopathy (HOCM) is inherited in an autosomal dominant manner with a high degree of penetrance. It is characterized by disproportionate hypertrophy of the interventricular septum. There is a corresponding reduction in compliance of the left ventricle with an increase in the end diastolic pressure. Contraction of the left ventricle causes obstruction of left ventricular outflow with a subsequent jerky rise in the pulse — this is associated with paradoxical anterior movement of the anterior leaflet of the mitral valve towards the septum. There is typically a double apex beat. The characteristic murmurs are a late aortic ejection systolic murmur which does not radiate to the neck, and a murmur of mitral regurgitation. Added 3rd and 4th heart sounds reflect the stiffness of the ventricle. There is no ejection click. A satisfactory stroke volume is dependent on maintaining ventricular volume and strategies to reduce this — e.g. increased contraction (digoxin, isoprenaline, exertion), reduced pre-load (Valsalva, squatting), or reduced afterload (nitrates and other vasodilators) — will cause a deterioration in function.

Investigations:
Chest X-ray — The left ventricle is prominent and may resemble the 'boot' shape of an aneurysm. The absence of post-stenotic dilatation helps differentiation from aortic stenosis.

ECG may show Q waves in inferior and lateral leads, increased R waves in septal leads, LVH, LBBB, and pre-excitation with a short PR interval and a slurred upstroke to the R wave resembling

Wolff-Parkinson-White syndrome.

An echocardiogram may show a small left ventricular cavity, a thick interventricular septum (> 1.3:1 ratio with the posterior left ventricular wall), paradoxical anterior movement of the anterior mitral leaflet in systole with delayed diastolic closure, and systolic closing of the aortic valves.

Ventricular arrhythmias are a common cause of sudden death and all patients should be assessed by 24 hour ECGs and given anti-arrhythmic therapy if indicated. Atrial fibrillation and sub-acute bacterial endocarditis may also occur. Beta blockers and verapamil may be beneficial for exertional symptoms by reducing obstruction.

30. SICK SINUS SYNDROME   BE

The sick sinus syndrome may occur at any age but is commonest in the elderly. It may be due to sino-atrial node fibrosis or degeneration, localized myocarditis, digoxin or quinidine toxicity, and may be associated with AV node dysfunction. Diphtheria may produce a similar condition. It is characterized by: inappropriate bradycardia; episodes of sinus arrest − often with no compensatory escape rhythm; a susceptibility to supraventricular tachyarrhythmias e.g. atrial fibrillation; and a tendency to delayed or absent return of sinus node activity following termination of a tachyarrhythmia. Syncopal episodes should be treated with a permanent pacemaker and this is an important precaution if anti-arrythmic drugs, particularly β-blockers and disopyramide, are administered as they predispose to sinus arrest. Systemic emboli occur in ≈15% of cases and, in the absence of contraindications, patients should be anticoagulated.

31. HODGKIN'S DISEASE   ABCDE

Hodgkin's disease typically affects the young/middle aged male. The four basic histological types are: lymphocyte predominant; lymphocyte depleted; mixed cellularity; and nodular sclerosing. The Reed-Sternberg cell is pathognomonic.

Clinical features include: lymphadenopathy − firm, rubbery and painless; hepatosplenomegaly; systemic symptoms — fever (including Pel-Ebstein), night sweats, weight loss; alcohol induced pain in involved tissue; pulmonary infiltrates; pathological fractures; cord compression; progressive multifocal leucoencephalopathy; opportunistic infections particularly reflect impaired cellular immunity (negative skin tests to recall antigens such as tuberculin and candida are usual).

Investigations may show:
    Haemoglobin — normocytic, normochromic anaemia is usual, but haemoglobin is often normal and haemolysis occasionally occurs
    White cell count — neutrophil leucocytosis and lymphopenia are common, and eosinophilia is seen in 10-15%. Lymphopenia correlates with active disease
    Platelets — thrombocytosis in active disease
    Bone marrow — rarely confirms infiltration
    Liver biochemistry may reflect hepatic infiltration.

Treatment is curative in the majority of cases (lymphocyte predominant stage IA having the best prognosis). Radiotherapy is administered for stages IA to IIIA and chemotherapy e.g. MOPP (for all 'B' disease and stages IIIA and IVA.

See February 1990 question 33.

32. CARPAL TUNNEL SYNDROME   **ABCD**

Most cases of carpal tunnel syndrome are idiopathic in fat middle aged women.

Other causes include:
    Pregnancy
    Pre-menstrually
    Oestrogen containing oral contraceptive pill
    Tenosynovitis (rheumatoid arthritis)
    Nephrotic syndrome
    Diabetes mellitus
    Acromegaly
    Multiple myeloma
    Haemodialysis

The association with long term dialysis is related to the accumulation of β-2 microglobulin, which is not dialysable by conventional cellulose-based membranes, and precipitates as amyloid deposits causing a characteristic arthropathy in these patients.

Symptoms and signs include: pain in the wrist which may radiate proximally (sic); paraesthesiae and anaesthesiae in the median three and a half fingers and the corresponding palm, and on occasions to ulnar nerve territory; and weakness of abductor pollicis brevis, flexor pollicis, adductor pollicis and opponens pollicis. Provocative tests (Tinel's sign, Phalen's test) have their advocates. Nerve conduction studies are useful where symptoms predominate and signs are scanty. Treatment is by decompression and treatment of any underlying cause.

33. DELAYED VISUAL PROVOKED POTENTIALS   AB

A flashing light, reversing chequerboard or other alternating pattern is used as the visual stimulus for visually evoked potentials (VEPs). The cortical response is measured with occipital cortical electrodes and the normal range for both latency and amplitude will vary according to conditions used.

Abnormal latencies are not confined to patients with multiple sclerosis and may also be seen in: glaucoma; optic nerve compression; vitamin B_{12} deficiency; and Friedreich's ataxia.

False positive diagnoses of MS ($\approx 10\%$ based on delayed VEPs alone) may be minimised by demonstrating an oligoclonal increase in CSF immunoglobulins.

Brainstem auditory evoked potentials (BAEPs)are achieved by a clicking stimulus at 65-70 dB above the hearing threshold in one ear whilst the other ear is masked. The seven resulting potentials, over a period of 10 ms, are designated I-VII and correspond to the afferent impulse arriving at different points in the auditory pathway. BAEPs are less useful than VEPs and abnormalities are present in MS, acoustic neuromas, brain stem disorders, Charcot-Marie-Tooth, alcoholism and uraemia.

Somatosensory evoked potentials are detected following electrical stimulation of a peripheral nerve, usually the median or tibial, over the appropriate sensory cortex. As with BAEPs, different components of the response correspond to the arrival of the impulse at different points of the afferent pathway. Abnormalities occur in multiple sclerosis as well as other degenerative conditions, but, unlike BAEPs, the changes are often very characteristic of the different conditions.

34. FRONTAL LOBE DAMAGE   AC

Signs of frontal lobe damage include: a personality change, grasp reflex, pout reflex and a positive palmo-mental reflex. Memory is predominantly a function of the temporal lobes and a receptive dysphasia of the post-central gyrus (Wernicke's area).

35. NORMAL PRESSURE HYDROCEPHALUS   ABCE

The aetiology of 'Normal pressure hydrocephalus' (NPH) is uncertain but it is assumed that *partial* obstruction of flow of CSF operates. It should be differentiated from cerebral atrophy, multiple infarcts, Alzheimer's disease and hypertensive encephalopathy though this is not possible on clinical grounds alone as all may have the characteristic features of dementia, gait disorder and urinary incontinence. A short history (with CT evidence of enlarging ventricles, periventricular translucency and relatively narrow cortical sulci) and/or a specific insult such as a head injury, meningitis or a sub-arachnoid haemorrhage make the diagnosis of NPH more likely but these circumstances are in the minority. The best predictive test for a beneficial outcome from surgery is measurement of outflow resistance — if this is < 11mm Hg/ml/minute then surgery is unlikely to be helpful.

36. AUTISM   ACE

The male:female ratio of autism is 4:1. The principal features are: onset before the age of 2.5 years of age; autistic aloneness — non-responsiveness to affection and stimulation and avoidance of eye-to-eye contact; language difficulties — mainly a cognitive abnormality, although up to 50% will eventually have *some* useful speech; repetitive behaviour, e.g. waggling hands in front of their eyes, and a desire for an unchanging environment; overactivity; 75% are educationally sub-normal; 25% experience seizures.

Although unusual in siblings, there is a familial element and increased concordance in monozygotic twins.

37. ANOREXIA NERVOSA   C

See February 1990 question 39 and June 1990 question 37.

38. SCHIZOPHRENIA   CDE

The features generally associated with a better prognosis in schizophrenia are those of typical acute schizophrenia and include: a good premorbid background including personality, psychosexual development, occupational history, and family and social relationships; older age; marriage; no previous psychiatric history; acute onset; rapid resolution; and presence of affective symptoms (i.e. disturbances of mood).

39. PSYCHIATRIC SYMPTOMS AND SYSTEMIC DISEASE   ABCDE

Cushing's syndrome — depression, euphoria or psychosis.

Myxoedema — cretinism in infants, depression, schizophreniform psychosis (myxoedema madness), and dementia.

Acute intermittent porphyria — depression, confusion and coma, and psychosis.

Vitamin B_{12} deficiency — progressive dementia.

Bronchial carcinoma — dementia is one of the characteristic non-metastatic manifestations of carcinoma.

40. COTTON WOOL SPOTS
ABCE

Cotton wool spots are seen in any cause of retinal infarction including: diabetes,HIV retinopathy, severe carotid occlusive disease, glaucoma, and in patients with anti-phospholipid antibodies. The lesions are smaller and have a shorter half life in HIV retinopathy compared with diabetes. Cotton wool spots are centered around the optic disc and usually disappear within a few weeks.

41. ASBESTOS EXPOSURE
BCD

The three main varieties of asbestos are chrysotile (white — this is the commonest type of asbestos and is also the least dangerous), crocidolite (blue) and amosite (brown). The potential consequences of asbestos exposure are:

i) asbestosis — parenchymal fibrosis may occur with all three types.
Clinical examination reveals fine end-expiratory basal crepitations and radiographs confirm lower lobe opacities. Lung function tests show a restrictive pattern with a reduction in gas transfer. The time of onset of the disease and the speed of progression are directly linked to the severity and duration of exposure

ii) pleural plaques are areas of fibrosis on the lower chest wall and diaphragmatic and pericardial surfaces. Calcification is common. There is no evidence of association with malignancy or progressive pleural disease

iii) benign pleural effusion

iv) pleural thickening may follow resolution of pleural effusions and, if extensive, may embarrass respiration

v) mesothelioma — painful tumour which may arise in pleural, peritoneal or pericardial mesothelium. The prognosis is poor and there is no effective treatment

vi) bronchial carcinoma — the incidence of carcinoma of the lung, especially adenocarcinoma and small cell is increased

See February 1990 question 26.

42. FARMER'S LUNG CD

See February 1990 question 44.

43. CYSTIC FIBROSIS BCDE

Cystic fibrosis is inherited in an autosomal recessive manner and is characterized by an abnormally low water content of exocrine gland secretions. Disease manifestations include:

Respiratory disease predominates — recurrent infection with progression to obstructive airways disease, bronchiectasis and cor pulmonale

Gastrointestinal — i) 'meconium ileus' in neonates gives way to constipation, rectal prolapse, intussusception and bouts of sub-acute obstruction, ii) pancreas — malabsorption with steatorrhoea.

Diabetes is a relatively late feature following recurrent attacks of pancreatitis

Liver — obstructive picture may progress to cirrhosis

Male infertility

The diagnosis is confirmed by demonstrating an increased (>60 mmol/l) Na^+ concentration in sweat (obtained by pilocarpine iontophoresis).

Treatment is mainly directed to the respiratory disorder with physiotherapy, postural drainage and aggressive treatment of pulmonary infections: *Pseudomonas aeruginosa* is the principal pathogen. There is evidence that expectoration of a more liquid, and therefore less tenacious, sputum may be achieved by either regular inhalation of amiloride or by using recombinant human DNA-ase (the rationale for the latter being the high concentration of DNA in these patients' sputum). A small proportion of these patients have now received heart/lung transplants. Pancreatic disease may require pancreatic enzymes, nutritional support and treatment for diabetes may be necessary.

44. METABOLIC ALKALOSIS

AC

The patient has a metabolic alkalosis with a compensatory, mild, respiratory acidosis manifesting as an increased serum HCO_3 and PCO_2. Hypokalaemia is a likely accompaniment.

The causes of this metabolic picture include:
Recurrent vomiting — due to loss of acid gastric contents
Administration of alkali
Cushing's syndrome
Conn's syndrome
Bartter's syndrome
Secretory villous adenoma
Drugs — diuretics, laxative abuse, carbenoxolone.

45. GUT PHYSIOLOGY

BCDE

Vasoactive intestinal polypeptide (VIP) is not confined to the gastro-intestinal tract where it is found in gland and neural cells. It is a powerful promoter of electrolyte and water secretion.

Gastric inhibitory peptidase (GIP) is secreted from the duodenal and jejunal mucosa in response to glucose and fats and, in turn, stimulates the release of insulin.

Secretin is produced by deep gland cells in the proximal small bowel in response to the presence of protein and acid. It stimulates the release of HCO_3 from the pancreas and, in association with cholecystokinin, promotes the secretion of pancreatic digestive enzymes.

Gastrin is produced by G cells (one of the APUD family of cells) in the antrum. It exists in various forms of which G17 has the most potent activity. Secretion is promoted by: stomach distension, protein, vagal discharge, calcium, adrenaline, and achlorhydria (e.g. high gastrin levels in pernicious anaemia). Acid, secretin, VIP, and GIP are all inhibitors of secretion. The main actions of gastrin are to stimulate the release of gastric acid and pepsin, and to promote growth of gastric mucosa. It also causes contraction of the oesophageal sphincter and stimulates insulin and glucagon secretion.

Cholera enterotoxin (specifically the A-1 subunit) stimulates the activity of adenylate cyclase in mucosal epithelial cells and the resulting increase in intracellular concentrations of cyclic AMP result in rapid excretion of electrolytes, and thus fluid, into the bowel lumen.

46. BARRETT'S OESOPHAGUS   C

Barrett's oesophagus is an acquired condition. Columnar epithelium forms in the lower oesophagus as a consequence of long standing acid reflux. Diagnosis is based on a combination of histology and confirmation of oesophageal origin, either by showing oesophageal motility on a barium swallow, or by measurement at endoscopy. The main symptoms are due to oesophagitis and, in some cases to the development of strictures. The condition is pre-malignant and regular monitoring with multiple biopsies is recommended.

47. HAEMOCHROMATOSIS   *recessive*   ABC

Haemochromatosis is an inborn error of metabolism manifesting as non-haem iron overload (haemosiderin and haemofuscin). Although broadly considered as inherited in an autosomal dominant fashion, penetrance is very variable and extreme manifestations are only common in homozygotes. Males are more commonly affected, probably because of the protective effect of menstruation in females. The gene is closely linked to the HLA A3 locus.

Clinical features include:
Diabetes
Slate grey skin pigmentation due to both iron and melanin
Cardiac failure — a common cause of death
Impotence
Arthropathy (pseudogout — chondrocalcinosis)
Cirrhosis with a marked incidence of hepatoma.

Iron studies show increased ferritin and saturated transferrin and histology of affected organs confirms iron deposition.

Treatment is serial venesection which improves both morbidity and mortality in the short term.

48. HELICOBACTER PYLORI   AC

Helicobacter pylori is a Gram negative micro-aerophilic bacillus. It possesses potent urease activity which may contribute to its pathogenicity. For all practical purposes it is confined to the stomach and duodenum (and occasionally in metaplastic (Barret's) oesophagus). Diagnosis is principally by culture and histology but a rapid, though less specific assay, based on urease activity may also be performed.

Transmission, based on epidemiological data only, is probably from person to person. It is present in ≈10% of asymptomatic 30 year olds and 60% of 60 year olds, and in virtually all patients with duodenal ulcers in whom it may be regarded as a necessary but not sufficient factor in the development of the DU. It is found in ≈80% of patients with gastric ulcers and a gastritis, confirmed histologically as an inflammatory infiltrate of the lamina propria, is virtually always present.

Effective treatment of *H. pylori* is difficult to prove. Bismuth preparations (e.g. De-Nol), but not H_2 antagonists or sucralfate, have some effect in a minority of patients and various combinations of antibiotics e.g. metronidazole +/- amoxil or tetracycline as well as bismuth may lead to eradication of the organism in ≈75% of cases for as long as 12 months. It is even more difficult to prove that eradication of *H. pylori* has any effect on symptoms in gastritis or on ulcer healing (mainly through problems with study design) though this is many groups' prejudice.

Another organism, *Gastrospirillum hominis,* has recently been described and is under investigation for a similar role in dyspepsia.

49. UNTREATED HYPERTENSION   ABC

Phaeochromocytoma accounts for ≈0.75% of cases of secondary hypertension. It may arise in any tissue of neuroectodermal origin but

90% are adrenal with the next most common site of origin in the Organ of Zuckerlandl in the aortic bifurcation. Phaeochromocytomas are known as the '10% tumours' as 10% are found outside the adrenal glands, 10% are bilateral and 10% are malignant. Familial cases are well recognized and these are almost wholly adrenal and often bilateral. Syndromes with which phaeochromocytoma are associated include: multiple endocrine neoplasia (MEN) II (autosomal dominant) — associated with medullary carcinoma of the thyroid gland, parathyroid adenoma or hyperplasia, and multiple neuromata on mucosal surfaces; and von Hippel Lindau syndrome — associated with retinal and cerebellar haemangioblastomas. The clinical manifestations are best remembered as: Pain — in chest and abdomen; Pallor; Perspiration; Polyuria — from glycosuria; hyPertension, often with diastolic and postural hyPotension; and Prostration.

Phaeochromocytomas are traditionally diagnosed by the presence of excess vanillylmandelic acid (VMA) in the urine, but more specific urinary assays of metadrenaline and metnoradrenaline are widely used (NB clonidine, methyl dopa, MAOIs, phenothiazines, bananas, tea, coffee and chocolate may all give artificially high readings). Plasma assays of adrenaline and nor-adrenaline (and also dopamine) are used in specialized centres. In all cases repeated assays may be necessary to confirm or refute the suspected diagnosis. Suppression tests may also aid diagnosis — a phaeochromocytoma prevents the normal suppression of adrenaline and nor-adrenaline following either an intravenous dose of pentolinium or an oral dose of clonidine. Localization of the tumour is best achieved by CT scanning. Lesions outside the adrenals, or where there is metastatic spread may be identified by isotope scintigraphy with I^{131} meta iodobenzyl-guanidine (MIBG) which localizes in adrenergic tissue. More invasive investigation e.g. arteriography and venous sampling, should be covered by both β and α blockade (of which α is the more important and should be started first — β blockade alone may increase (sic) the blood pressure).

Surgery is the treatment of choice. Medical management of malignant cases, which are characteristically indolent, with phenoxybenzamine is often very successful. α methyl tyrosine, which inhibits the production of adrenaline and nor-adrenaline by preventing the hydroxylation of tyrosine to DOPA, may also be used.

An abdominal bruit suggests renal artery stenosis. 5-hydroxy-indoleacetic acid is the metabolite of 5-OH tryptophan (serotonin) and its presence in excess in the urine suggests the carcinoid syndrome.

50. HYPERTHYROIDISM   BCE

Hyperthyroidism is associated with amenorrhoea and hypothyroidism with menorrhagia. Difficulty in climbing stairs is due to a proximal myopathy.

In addition to the typical manifestations, rare features of hyperthyroidism include: choreoathetosis, hypercalcaemia, telangiectasiae, palmar erythema, steatorrhoea and an increase in blood volume with consequent hypoalbuminaemia.

Nocturnal parathesiae in the hands is a feature of carpal tunnel syndrome, a recognized complication of hypothyroidism.

51. SECONDARY AMENORRHOEA   BDE

Always consider pregnancy and menopause in the differential diagnosis of secondary amenorrhoea!

The major causes of amenorrhoea may be divided into:
  Hypothalamic-pituitary disease — including the many causes of
      hyperprolactinaemia
  Gonadal disease — ovarian failure of any cause will be suggested
      by a high FSH which will often be accompanied by an increased
      LH (an increased LH alone suggests polycystic ovary
      syndrome)
  Adrenal disease — including Cushing's disease and virilization
  Thyroid disease — both hyper- and hypothyroidism)
  Mechanical causes

Clomiphene is an anti-oestrogen which stimulates gonadotrophin release by inhibiting the action of gonadal steroids on the hypothalamus. It is typically used in the Stein-Leventhal syndrome.

Kallman's syndrome is a cause of primary amenorrhoea.

A number of organ specific auto-immune diseases including Addison's disease, ovarian failure, pernicious anaemia, hypo-parathyroidism, Grave's disease, Hashimoto's disease, Type I diabetes, coeliac disease and myasthenia gravis occur together with increased frequency.

52. CROHN'S DISEASE   BE

Crohn's disease has well recognized associations with erythema nodosum and pyoderma gangrenosum.

Dermatitis herpetiformis is associated with coeliac disease.

Lupus pernio is a feature of sarcoidosis.

53. HAEMODIALYSIS   DE

Erythropoietin is able to increase the haemoglobin to the normal range but this is not necessary and in any event is often precluded by the development of hypertension. The shortening of the bleeding time is similar to that demonstrated following blood transfusions and has not yet been explained.

Continuous monitoring of dialysate (electrical conductivity) ensures that haemolysis in the extracorporeal circuit does not occur.

Aluminium toxicity causes an Fe-deficient picture. Serum ferritin may be normal in dialysis patients despite functional iron deficiency.

54. DIABETIC NEPHROPATHY   E

Up to 50% of diabetic patients will develop nephropathy after 40 years and it is particularly common in some non-caucasoid races. Mortality in this group of patients is up to 100 times greater than diabetic patients without nephropathy. The earliest clinical evidence (i.e. micro-albuminuria) occurs at least 5 years after the diagnosis of diabetes and at this stage there is no increase in the serum creatinine concentration. The characteristic features of frank diabetic nephropathy as the cause of renal failure are: proteinuria (with an inactive urinary sediment), hypertension and other evidence of diabetic microvascular disease, especially retinopathy. The absence of any of these three features should increase the suspicion of an alternative cause for renal failure.

Diabetes is the classical cause of chronic renal failure with normal sized kidneys, other conditions giving this appearance include multiple myeloma, sarcoidosis and lymphoproliferative disorders.

The mainstay of management of diabetic nephropathy is scrupulous control of hypertension. There is accumulating evidence that ACE inhibitors, by virtue of reducing renal hyper-perfusion, have a particular protective effect over and above their antihypertensive properties. (Ca antagonists may also have a protective effect in CRF generally by reducing interstitial calcification.) There is no consensus that improved diabetic control is beneficial in these patients, but there is at least epidemiological evidence that this may be the case. Low protein diets have their advocates but the hyperfiltration theory (of Brenner) has fallen into disrepute to some extent.

A [HCO3] of > 20 mmol/l would be expected in someone with this degree of renal failure of any aetiology, assuming no specific tubular disorder (see explanation Q 55 of June 1990 paper).

55. MEMBRANOUS NEPHROPATHY   BC

Most cases of membranous nephropathy (MN) are idiopathic and are associated with HLA DR3. The prognosis can be considered in thirds i.e. 1/3 get better, 1/3 remain nephrotic, and 1/3 progress to end-stage renal failure. Progression of disease in this latter group may be ameliorated by a six month course of alternating months of high dose steroid and chlorambucil therapy ('Ponticelli' regime) but management is otherwise that of the nephrotic state. Most cases of secondary MN are due to drugs i.e. penicillamine, gold salts and captopril, and a third group are those related to solid malignancies — typically of the bronchus and bowel. SLE may cause any renal histology and MN associated with SLE is now designated Type V

See February 1990 question 55.

56. SECONDARY SYPHILIS   ACD

The major features of secondary syphilis, which usually manifest 6-8 weeks after the primary lesion, are:
  Skin lesions — the rash is characteristically widespread, symmetrical, non-irritating macular, and less commonly, papular. It tends to be centripetal, but a centrifugal distribution, i.e. on the face and soles, increases the probability of syphilis as the cause.
  Condylomata lata may be found in moist areas, including perineal, perianal, axillary and sub-mammary regions, and are highly infectious
  Oral mucosal lesions — including characteristic nail track ulcers — are painless and are also highly infectious
  Generalised lymphadenopathy, which is painless.

Rarer manifestations include:
  Meningitis — typically low grade
  Alopecia
  Laryngitis
  Hepatitis
  Nephrotic syndrome — usually with membranous histology
  Periostitis
  Anterior uveitis

57. NORMAL MILESTONES   CDE

The baby will support its head from about 12-16 weeks (though will not sit unaided until about 26 weeks).

The moro reflex is abduction and extension of the arms following a small 'drop' of the baby's head whilst it is held at 45°. The reflex disappears after 2-3 months.

The palmar grasp reflex has disappeared by 2-3 months.

At six months, the baby will still be grasping with two hands, finger and thumb grasping only appearing at 9 months.

Hand dominance is not established until ≈2, and sometimes not until 4, years of age.

58. DOWN'S SYNDROME   **CDE**

See February 1990 question 58.

59. NEONATAL RESPIRATORY DISTRESS SYNDROME   **CE**

The neonatal respiratory distress syndrome has a variety of causes including: increased pulmonary pressure and blood flow e.g. in patent ductus arteriosus; reduced plasma protein concentration; high airway pressures e.g. ventilation; high oxygen concentrations; and surfactant deficiency. Pre-term infants are more susceptible for a variety of reasons, including deficiency of surfactant (which may be assessed at amniocentesis by the lecithin:sphingomyelin ratio), and a deficiency of elastase and α1-anti-trypsin inhibitors: proteases are thought to increase the permeability of the lungs.

60. OSTIUM SECUNDUM ATRIAL SEPTAL DEFECT   **BDE**

Ostium secundum defects are usually asymptomatic in childhood. The clinical signs of an uncomplicated case include: an absent left ventricular impulse; wide fixed splitting of the second heart sound with a loud pulmonary component of the second heart sound; a pan-systolic pulmonary flow murmur and a soft tricuspid diastolic flow murmur; ECG shows right axis deviation, partial right bundle-branch-block, and right ventricular hypertrophy. Chest radiograph shows mild cardiomegaly, a small aortic knuckle and prominent pulmonary artery with pulmonary plethora.

Symptoms usually develop progressively from middle adult life, firstly with atrial arrhythmias, including AF, and later with right heart failure.

INDEX OF TOPICS

Hypertrophic cardiomyopathy 106
Hyperuricaemia 22
Hypocalcaemia 94
Hypokalaemic acidosis 4
Hypokalaemic alkalosis 53
Hyponatraemia 3
Hypophosphataemia 8
Hypothyroidism 82
Immunoglobulins 10, 58
Industrial lung disease 24
Infant development 89, 121
Infectious mononucleosis 99
Insect vectors 60
Insulin 7
Insulinoma 35
Intellectual deterioration 35
Iron 64
Jaundice, drug induced 20
Leg ulceration 92
Lithium 87
Macrocytosis 101
Maternal
  cytomegalovirus 12
  rubella 12
  toxoplasma 12
Medullary cystic disease 6
Medullary sponge kidney 5
Membranous nephropathy 120
Mental handicap 75
Metabolic alkalosis 114
Methaemoglobinaemia 1
Mitral valve prolapse 68
MMR vaccine 12, 59
Mood 74
Multiple myeloma 9
Multiple sclerosis 72
Mycoplasma pneumoniae 75
Neonatal respiratory distress
  syndrome 122
Nephrotic syndrome 45
Neurotransmitters 56
Non steroidal anti-inflammatory
  drugs 103
Normal pressure hydrocephalus 110
Obesity, childhood 47
Optic neuritis 72
Orchioblastoma 90
Ostium secundum 122
Papilloedema 47
Paraprotein 9
Parasitic infection, pulmonary 98
Parasuicide 34
Parkinson's disease 71
Parkinson's syndrome 103
Parotid swelling 53
Pellagra 78
Photosensitivity 65
Pleural effusion 37

Pneumoconiosis 24
Polycystic kidney disease
  adult 5
  infantile 5
Polymyalgia rheumatica 31
Porphyria, acute intermittent 17
Post-streptococcal
  glomerulonephritis 85
PR interval 70
Primary biliary cirrosis 79
Pruritus 85
Pseudomembranous colitis 13
Puberty 91
QT interval 105
Radial nerve 94
Renal tubular acidosis, distal 4
Renal tubule physiology 56
Retinal infarction 112
Rheumatoid arthritis 104
Salmonella 14
Sarcoidosis 36
 chizophrenia 111
Scurvy 67
Second heart sound 28
Seventh nerve 7
SIADH 4, 77
Sick sinus syndrome 107
Sickle cell disease 62, 67
Sixth cranial nerve 55
Skeletal abnormalities 67
Sodium valproate 102
Spinal cord transection 6
Splenectomy 70
Statistics 23, 66, 104
Subarachnoid haemorrhage 33, 71
Syphilis 35, 121
Systemic disease, cutaneous
  markers 52
Systemic lupus erythematosus 26
Systemic sclerosis 104
Thiamine deficiency 35
Thiazide diuretics 102
Thrombocytopenia 61
Toxoplasma gondii 98
Toxoplasmosis 98
Tricyclic antidepressants 64, 96
Trigeminal neuralgia 33
Tuberculosis 11
Typhoid 100
Ulcerative colitis 39
Urine, abnormal colouration 45
Uveitis 11, 92
Vibration sense 73
Vitiligo 52
Wilson's disease 39
Wolff-Parkinson-White syndrome 69
X-linked recessive diseases 54